A STUDY OF THE MILLENNIAL REIGN

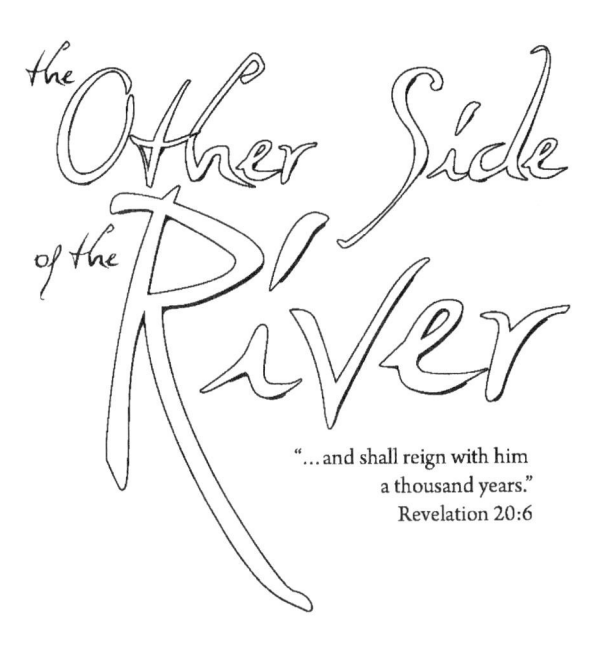

the Other Side of the River

"...and shall reign with him a thousand years."
Revelation 20:6

Dr. James Wilkins

*What will be your **mailing address** on this earth for 1000 years?*

A STUDY OF THE MILLENNIAL REIGN

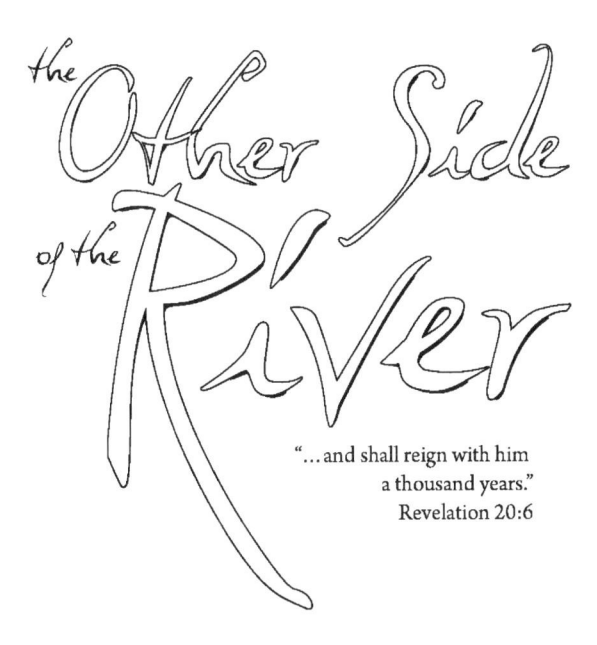

the Other Side of the River

"...and shall reign with him
a thousand years."
Revelation 20:6

Dr. James Wilkins

*What will be your **mailing address**
on this earth for 1000 years?*

Copyright © 2009 Dr. James Wilkins. All rights reserved.

Writings contained herein are by the author unless otherwise stated.

No part of this publication may be reproduced, stored in a retrieval system or transmitted in any way by any means—electronic, mechanical, photocopy, recording or otherwise—without the prior permission of the copyright holder, except as provided by USA copyright law.

Printed in the United States of America.

All Scriptures are taken from the King James Bible.

ISBN # 978-1-935075-56-1

Printed by Calvary Publishing
A Ministry of Parker Memorial Baptist Church
1902 East Cavanaugh Road, Lansing, Michigan 48910
www.CalvaryPublishing.org

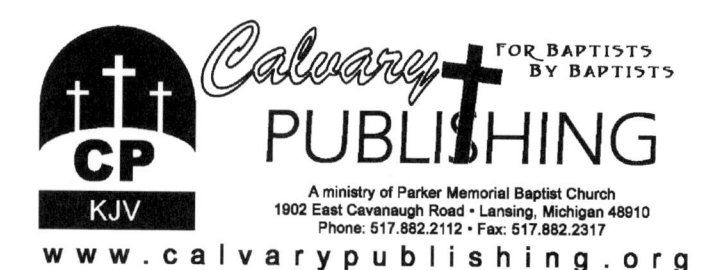

Calvary PUBLISHING
FOR BAPTISTS BY BAPTISTS
CP KJV
A ministry of Parker Memorial Baptist Church
1902 East Cavanaugh Road • Lansing, Michigan 48910
Phone: 517.882.2112 • Fax: 517.882.2317
www.calvarypublishing.org

Samuel Stennett referred to the Jordan River as death and wrote

On Jordan's stormy banks I stand,
And cast a wishful eye
To Canaan's fair and happy land,
Where my possessions lie.

I am bound for the promised land,
Oh who will come and go with me?
I am bound for the promised land.

Many may lament and sing.

On Jordan's stormy bank I stand
And cast a **tearful eye**
At Canaan's bleak and lonely hand
Where scarce a possession lie

I am bound for the Promised land
Oh God, help me as I journey all alone,
I am bound for the promised land.

If you failed to obey God's command of **Lay up for yourselves treasures in heaven** you face a bleak Millennium.

This book reveals God's way to change your mailing ADDRESS FOR 1000 YEARS.

Forward

As I attempt to write on the subject of the Millennial Reign, I do it with much reluctance.

I felt that God was prompting me to write on the Millennium, but I delayed beginning. After a heart attack and two strokes, I knew I had better start before I died. I wrote the first chapter and published it as a small booklet entitled, *"Thy Kingdom Come."* I continued writing the manuscript which turned out to be over two hundred pages. I then put it away in a drawer where it stayed for over two years. After that period I brought it back out and read it.

There is still so much that we do not know about the general subject of the Kingdom. There is still so much that I do not know about the Millennium. But there are some things I do know, and there are other things I am pretty sure of. One thing that I am sure of is that the truths I know about the Millennium will help some people. Some of the things I know **will spark people to study more** about the coming King, who will usher in His Millennial Kingdom.

So it is with fear and trembling that I present *THE OTHER SIDE OF THE RIVER.*

The main purpose for the doctrine of the Millennium is to stimulate and motivate people **for an all out effort to witness to the six and one-half to seven billion people** who live on our planet. We must make every effort to tell them about a loving Saviour and His provisions for them.

The title of the book, *The Other Side of the River,* may be more appropriate if we ask the question, **"Where will you live on the other side of the River?"** The Bible absolutely teaches that what a child of God does for the Lord in this three score and ten phase of his life **will dictate where he will live on the other side of the river during the 1000-year reign.**

If this writing will convince people of that one truth, your author will have achieved a major part of what he hoped to accomplish in presenting *The Other Side of the River.*

Table of Contents

Chapter One   **page 13**
       "THY KINGDOM COME"
     Chapter one teaches the millennial kingdom is God's method of motivating Christians. As such they are to look and pray daily for its coming.

Chapter Two   **page 48**
    THE SUBJECTS OF THE KINGDOM
     In the Kingdom there will be two classes of citizens. Those who and reign with Christ and those who forfeited their inheritance and are subjects. It identifies how one can qualify to rule with Him.

Chapter Three   **page 63**
         **OUR GLORIFIED
     BODIES IN THE KINGDOM**
     This chapter examines the different types of bodies that people will receive at his coming.

Chapter Four   **page74**
     LAWS OF PROFIT AND LOSS
     This chapter proves that how a person lives their life now will dictate where they will live for 1000 years in the millennium.

Chapter Five   **page 104**
  **THOSE WHO WILL BE TRANSFERRED
        INTO THE KINGDOM**
     People from the sheep nations will survive the tribulation period and will be transferred into the kingdom in their natural bodies.

Chapter Six   page 118
ETERNAL LIFE IS A GIFT, REWARDS ARE EARNED
This chapter shows the differences in eternal life (a gift) and earning a reward (by works)

Chapter Seven   page 131
THOSE WHO WILL TRIUMPH IN THE KINGDOM
People by their faith and service will earn a position of honor for 1000 years. There are twelve different positions of reward studied.

Chapter Eight   page 169
THOSE WHO WILL SHED TEARS IN THE KINGDOM! - PART A
We note the pain and suffering of some who will live a 1000 years with "ashes only". We note the heartbreak and tears of those who will live a 1000 years with "something worse than death.

Chapter Nine   page 195
THOSE WHO WILL SHED TEARS IN THE KINGDOM! - PART B
Chapter nine is a continuation of tears that some will shed for 1000 years. **The preacher who will plow for 1000 years**. Instead of sharing in Christ eternal glory he will work as a slave. **A poisonous servant cast into outer darkness.** Light symbolizes fellowship while darkness symbolizes being out of fellowship.

Chapter Ten   **page 222**
A PLEADING CALL TO THE ELEVENTH HOUR CHRISTIANS

Jesus, as Lord of the harvest, offers the nominal believer living today a way to redeem his life and earn a full reward in the millennial.

Chapter Eleven   **page 256**
THE PURPOSE OF THE KINGDOM PRINCIPLE

This principle is all but hidden from this 21st century and its great motivational benefits.

Chapter Twelve   **page 269**
THE CARROT THAT DOMINATES THE OTHER SIDE OF THE RIVER

A more in-depth study of the motivational value of the coming 1000 year kingdom

Chapter Thirteen   **page 292**
PETER'S PEN

This chapter shows how Apostle Peter and Paul motivated their disciples.

Chapter Fourteen   **page 321**
THE GLORY BEYOND THE SUNSET PICTURES YOUR COMING DAY

This chapter shows you, the reader, how to incorporate these motivating principles into your life.

EPILOGUE   **page 341**
ABOUT THE AUTHOR   **page 343**
BOOKS BY THE AUTHOR   **page 345**

Chapter One
"THY KINGDOM COME"

The next dispensation, which follows our present age, is **the Millennial Reign of Christ**. We could be in that glorious age before the fellow that bought that luxurious new SUV today has it paid off. He was placed on the **seven-year** payment plan because of his good credit record.

When Jesus comes back as a thief in the night to rapture His saints, the saved will go to the Judgment Seat of Christ and to the great Rewards Banquet. On earth, the Great Tribulation will begin and the last half of the seven-year period will be so horrible that no flesh will survive, except those days be shortened. That's right, no flesh or human being will survive all of the catastrophes that will conclude with the Battle of Armageddon, **unless those days** (seven years) shall be shortened. (Matt 24:22)

IT IS TIME TO START THINKING ABOUT THE KINGDOM

There are at least four reasons why you should begin to think about the coming 1000-year reign.

Time Could Be Very Short

It may not be in seven years, but then again, it could be. We don't know. In fact, no one knows the day and hour of His return except God, the Father.

> Anything with the potential of being so sudden and dramatic should occupy your mind and concern.

Nor do we know what position we will hold in the Millennial Kingdom. This statement is directed to the saved only, because a non-Christian has a very small chance of ever escaping the Tribulation and seeing the Millennium. **Anything with the potential of being so sudden** and dramatic should concern you and occupy your mind.

Upon Graduation You Will Move There

Death is described as a graduation for the child of God. Death, to the child of God, is the servant who ushers him into the presence of God in Heaven. Since we move from time into **a land that is eternal**, it is my opinion that it will seem but a very short time before we go to the Bema Stand (Judgment Seat of Christ), and then into the Millennium. **Your graduation could happen before** the fellow with the good credit record makes his first payment or his last. We have no assurance of how long we will live. But we know that, **"...It is appointed unto men once to die, but after this the judgment:"** Hebrews 9:27

You Will Live There 1000 Years

An old gospel song pictures someone standing on Jordan's stormy banks (death) and casting a wishful eye. He is looking, according to the song, to Canaan Land (Heaven) where his possessions lie.

> Death divides your present life from your future life.

Think about this. Death divides your present life from your future life. You have a few years on this side of death and **1000 years on the other side of death**. It will be at least 1000 years before you will go **into eternal Heaven**, where you will not have a vivid memory of your present life with its deeds and misdeeds. Your memory will be changed **after** the Great White Throne Judgment (for the lost), which will happen at the end of the Millennium. (Rev 20:1-12) God will then create a new Heaven and a new earth. When this happens, **He will wipe all tears away** and, **"...the former things are passed away." Rev 21:4** Until that happens, our memories will live with

the commendation or rebuke that Jesus gives us at the Judgment Seat.

The law of big numbers, which the insurance companies use to compute mortality tables, says that a man of average health will live approximately 82.4 years.

> What makes more sense – worrying about this short journey **to the river** or your long-term career **on the other side of the river**?

Your writer is, as of this writing, 78 years old. Using their numbers and "the river" as a symbol of death, he has a little less than four years **on this side** of death. According to the Bible, he has 1000 years to live **on the other side** of the river.

What Job Should You Worry About?

What makes more sense – worrying about this short journey **to the river** or your long-term career **on the other side of the river**? God has already promised (in Matt 6:33) that if one will seek first the Kingdom of God, then He will supply all his needs. Your Heavenly Father has promised to help you as you serve **as the steward over your short life on this earth**. He even stated that it is His (God's) good pleasure to aid and help you while you labor to fulfill your purpose.

But your papa, our Heavenly Father, the mighty creator of Heaven and earth, really wants you to have a good position for the complete 1000-year reign when His son, Jesus, is the world's boss. Remember, what you do during this short stay on the earth **will determine** where you will live and what you will be doing for the full 1000 years.

> Remember, what you do during this short stay on the earth **will determine** where you will live and what you will be doing for the full 1000 years.

THE PROMINENCE OF THE KINGDOM

The question, "What position will you occupy in His Kingdom?" **startles people, but it shouldn't**. It was something early Christians thought about. Two of the apostles even sent their mother to request that they might sit on either side of Jesus during His 1000-year reign. Their request caused great dissension and brought rebuke from Jesus, but it shows that early followers of Jesus were already thinking about the soon coming Kingdom.

Pray For the Kingdom To Come

Not only did the disciples think about the coming 1000-year reign, but Jesus taught them, and all Christians, to pray for the coming Kingdom.

"Thy kingdom come. Thy will be done in earth, as it is in Heaven." Matthew 6:10 The youngest little Sunday school child recognizes that expression as one which is found in the

> We all commanded to pray everyday for the coming millennial kingdom

Lord's (model) prayer. It is probably one of the first prayers a child is taught to pray. **"...Our Father, which art in heaven, Hallowed be thy name. Thy kingdom come..." Matthew 6:9-10**

That is not just a beautiful little saying that sounds good, but it is a command by our Savior to pray for His soon coming Kingdom. He knew that if we prayed for the coming Kingdom, we would have a greater possibility of living our lives **in the light of that coming kingdom and eternity**. We would live our lives focused on the coming world instead of being so involved in the present world all around us, which will soon pass away.

Look Toward the Kingdom To Come

The very first sermon Jesus preached was about the coming Kingdom, **"...Repent: for the kingdom of heaven is at hand." Matthew 4:17**

For the first three years of His ministry, He offered the literal Kingdom to Israel. He did everything to prove to the Jews that He was their promised Messiah. The Jews marveled at His knowledge and the power of His preaching, as He used the Scriptures to prove that He was "the great **I AM**" and their coming Messiah.

His miracles proved He was the supernatural God that had come to the earth wrapped in human flesh. Although the common man was convinced, the Jewish leaders refused to accept these infallible miracles and truths, and rejected Him.

In **Matthew 16:20**, He charged His disciples not to preach anymore that He was the Christ, or Messiah. The Jews, in their unbelief, had rejected Him and His offer to establish the Kingdom.

In the next verse, He began to prepare the apostles' minds for His soon coming death on the cross. As the Jewish leaders became more hostile and vocal concerning their plan to kill Him, the crowds of those who were brave enough to be seen openly in His meetings became smaller and smaller.

The apostles, being human, began to doubt and question His leadership. Peter, as their spokesman, was provoked to come right out and ask Jesus, "Behold, we have forsaken [left] all, and followed thee; **what shall we have therefore?" Matt 19:27**

Jesus calmly answered them that their paycheck for **all of their sacrificial service was to rule the earth in the coming 1000 year Kingdom. (Matt 19:28-29)**

In **Luke 22:29-30**, Luke gave the plainest statement of Jesus' teaching about the Kingdom to the apostles. Jesus promised them, "And I appoint unto you a kingdom, as my Father hath appointed unto me; That ye may **eat and drink at my table in my kingdom, and sit on thrones judging the twelve tribes of Israel**."

Through the stress and unexpected events (His crucifixion) that followed shortly afterward, this promise seemed to have escaped the apostles.

Upon His resurrection, Jesus spent the **last forty days** of His ministry, before going back to Heaven, preaching and teaching about the coming Kingdom. Note this great truth as revealed in **Acts 1:3, "…being seen of them forty days, and speaking of the things pertaining to the kingdom of God:"**

This teaching concerning the coming Kingdom, where the twelve apostles would eat and drink at His table and sit upon thrones judging the twelve tribes of Israel, led the apostles in the last service before He ascended to ask this question, "…Lord, wilt thou **at this time** restore again the kingdom to Israel?" Acts 1:6

Jesus informed them that it was not for them to know **the times or seasons**. (Acts 1:7) It wasn't the thing they should concern themselves with at that time. There were only two things that they should be concerned about.

First, they were to wait in prayer and **be empowered by the Holy Spirit**.

Second, they were to give themselves over fully **to spreading the Gospel to every creature** in Jerusalem, Judea, Samaria, and to the uttermost parts of the earth.

Jesus' exact comment to them was, "But ye **shall receive power**, after that the Holy Ghost is come upon you: and **ye shall be witnesses** unto me both in Jerusalem, and

Judaea, and in Samaria, and unto the uttermost part of the earth." Acts 1:8

Based on accomplishing these two simple commandments – being empowered by the Holy Spirit and then going into all the world – He would fulfill His promise of **letting them help Him** rule the earth in the coming Kingdom.

That promise of being a king and sitting on one of the twelve thrones of Israel **focused the apostles' minds** on that future day, and they never lost that focus. They constantly looked for the second coming of Jesus, which would usher in the Kingdom.

> They constantly looked for the second coming of Jesus, which would usher in the Kingdom.

Work Toward the Kingdom To Come

There were two things that were to be utmost on the apostles' minds as they led in their worldwide effort of evangelism. They were to be focused on getting the Gospel to every creature in the world, and on His second coming to establish His Kingdom.

They were to make a clear presentation of the plan of salvation to save lost sinners. They were to convince sinners of God's love and provision for every man. In doing so, they were warned that they would encounter hostility and

> Jesus became even more connected and involved with His disciples **in times of danger** and persecution.

possible death. On one occasion, Jesus told them that He was sending them as **lambs among wolves**. (Luke 10:3) He was quick to assure them of His continual presence and protection. On another occasion, He said, "I will never leave you nor forsake you." On the final day of His earthly ministry, He literally assured them, "I will be with you perpetually, on every occasion until the close and consummation of the age." (Matt 28:20)

In the first major persecution against the church, Saul of Tarsus caused many of the members to be put in jail or put to death. When Saul was struck down in conviction on the road to Damascus, Jesus asked him, "Saul, Saul, **why persecutest thou me?**" Acts 9:4   Paul was persecuting the Christians, but Jesus took the persecution of His saints **as if it was being personally directed to Him**. That statement illustrates how close the fellowship was that Jesus and His followers enjoyed.

Jesus became even more connected and involved with His disciples **in times of danger** and persecution. When the man who had been crippled for thirty-eight years was healed, the authorities became very hostile and threatening to the apostles. They brought John and Peter into court. As they observed the behavior and countenance of these two apostles, **Jesus' presence seemed to shine through them.** The authorities took note and found, according to their standards, that the apostles were **ignorant and unlearned men**. Then the Bible says a strange thing, "…they took knowledge of them, **that they had been with Jesus.**" Acts 4:13   In times of serious trouble, Jesus was with them and the authorities could tell.

When Stephen was stoned to death, Heaven was opened and he could see Jesus looking down in concern. Then the Bible declares that the members of the council literally stared at the face of this dying man and "…saw his face as it had been the face of an angel." Acts 6:15   When Jesus promised his disciples, "Lo, I will be with you always," it was not an idle promise. God's children can expect Jesus to get in the fiery furnace with them as He did with the three Hebrew children so many years ago.

The close, endearing, and personal fellowship that Jesus shared with his disciples in times of persecution and suffering is, no doubt, why **Paul desired the fellowship of His suffering**.

They were to get the message of hope concerning the sacrificial death of Jesus to every person regardless of **any personal pain and suffering**. The salvation of sinners had cost Jesus His life. There was **never a more shameful** treatment of a human being, than what Jesus suffered.

Why did He suffer? He suffered in order to save people from hell. On more than one occasion, He reminded the disciples that **the servant was no better than their master**. If He had given His all to get people saved, then He expected the same from them. They were to **work zealously** until His return, or until their death.

His Coming Meant Rewards in the Kingdom

The second thing that was to be utmost in their minds was His imminent return to earth as the King.

As the apostles were saying goodbye to Jesus and staring up into the heavens where He had just disappeared, they were reassured by two angels who said, "Why stand ye gazing up into heaven? This same Jesus, which is taken up from you into heaven, **shall so come in like manner** as ye have seen him go into heaven." Acts 1:11 How this experience must have burned in their memories and kept them **looking up for the rest of their lives**!

> *"In my Father's house are many mansions: if it were not so, I would have told you*

The night before His crucifixion, Jesus gave them the promise that has blessed the whole world through the centuries. "In my Father's house are many mansions: if it were not so, I would have told you. I go to prepare a place for you. And if I go and prepare a place for you, **I will come again**, and receive you unto myself; that where I am, there ye may be also." John 14:2-3

This personal promise of His coming back for them, given on the last night of His life on the earth, must have always been prominent in their minds. They must have reasoned, "**If God created the Heavens and the earth in six days**, then just how long will it take Jesus to create some mansions?" How they must have treasured and been inspired by the final service with their precious friend and Savior, and **the promise of His second coming**!

They would eat at His table. On His return, they would have personal fellowship with Him and eat at His table. His personal promise to them was, "That ye may eat and drink at my table in my kingdom…" Luke 20:30

> Can't you see how that promise kept them going in spite of their pain and suffering? They could always get up in the morning and say, "**This may be the day of His coming!**"

Can't you see how that promise kept them going in spite of their pain and suffering? They could always get up in the morning and say, "**This may be the day of His coming!**" As they faced martyrdom and watched their persecutors prepare for their executions, they could rejoice and say, "**This is the day!** I have won! I will get my throne and eat at Jesus' table for 1000 years!"

THEY WERE ASSURED OF ABSOLUTE SUCCESS

Not only did they have a perfect teacher who instructed them of the truths of

God's perfect Word, they had **a perfect role model to follow and imitate**.

He Washed Their Feet

By this simple act, He demonstrated that they were to serve others. Paul amplified this principle when he wrote, **"Let nothing be done through strife or vain glory; but in lowliness of mind let each esteem other better than themselves. Look not every man on his own things, but every man also on the things of others."** Phil 2:3-4 As they imitated His servant leadership, it kept them from having conflict with each other.

> He that **"will be chief** among you, let him **be your servant..."** Matt 20:27

Jesus' Example of Humility

Jesus was God, but He took on the form of a man. As a man, He humbled Himself, even to die on the cross, **the lowest act of self-abasement and humility that could be shown**. The Scripture states that because of the giving up of Himself to die on the cross, "Jesus was given a name above every name and that all the world will **bow before him** and confess His Lordship."

The lesson the apostles learned was this. "Let this mind be in you, which was also in Christ Jesus:" Phil 2:5 He that "...**will be chief** among you, let him **be your servant:**" Matt 20:27

It was very clear by Jesus' example that the ones who will be the greatest in the soon coming Kingdom will be the ones who humble themselves in faithful execution of their service to Jesus, even if it meant death. All of the apostles died a martyr's death except John who, as an old man in his nineties, gave the world **the book of victories**, called the Book of Revelation.

Those Personal Promises Transformed The Apostles

Examine the lives of the apostles before the resurrection of Christ and the empowering of the Holy Spirit. **They were scared, confused and disorganized**. They were even hiding behind locked doors. They had heard that Jesus was alive, but the fact hadn't become a reality yet. They also had been promised a future place of glory in the coming Kingdom, but they hadn't caught the impact of that promise either. **It was all just a bunch of words**. But forty days with Jesus and the empowering of the Holy Spirit

TRANSFORMED THEM INTO MEN **WHOSE COURSE COULD NOT BE CHANGED OR STOPPED**.

Part of their power came from the filling of the Holy Spirit. But great services, such as the ones they experienced on and after the Day of Pentecost, could only carry them so far. The promises concerning the future Kingdom could, and would, carry them all the way through their lives.

> The promises concerning the future Kingdom could, and would, carry them all the way through their lives.

If they endured hardships, then their positions would become even better because, "If we suffer, we shall also reign with him...." II Tim 2:12 The other promise states that the more one suffers, the greater the eternal glory will be. "For our **light affliction**, which is but for a moment, worketh for us a far more exceeding and **eternal weight of glory**." II Cor 4:17

If they were martyred, then they would have their place in the future Kingdom **plus**

> The apostles knew they would die. It was only a matter of **when, how, and for whom**. They chose to give their lives for a **sure thing**, to obtain the promise of Jesus.

the crown of life, which is one of the

supreme rewards. "...I will give thee a crown of life." Rev 2:10

The apostles understood their jobs. They were to get the gospel to every creature in the whole world, regardless of what it might cost them personally.

They understood their reward, "to eat and drink at the Master's table" as they were ruling and reigning with King Jesus. **But little did they know** that parts of **that Holy City would be named in their honor** by their grateful Lord. *(Rev 21:14)*

They Traded What They Couldn't Keep

The apostles, along with every person since Adam, couldn't keep their lives. They all died (except Enoch and Elijah). All of the millions of people since the apostles have also died, regardless of what they did to prolong their lives. The apostles knew they would die. It was only a matter of **when, how, and for whom**. They chose to give their lives for a **sure thing,** to obtain the promise of Jesus.

> The apostles understood their jobs. They were to get the gospel to every creature in the whole world, regardless of what it might cost them personally.

For Something They Could Not Lose

The absolute promise of Jesus to the apostles, that if they gave their lives to get people saved then He would give them a throne and a position to eat and drink at His table during the 1000-year Kingdom, **transformed them**.

> They traded what they could not keep (their lives) for something they will never lose – **God's glory, commendation and eternal fellowship**.

They were raised from a small spot on the earth, working at nominal jobs, and elevated to one of the top positions in the Millennial Reign and eternal age. They traded what they could not keep (their lives) for something they would never lose – **God's glory, commendation, and eternal fellowship**.

They labored for Christ and His Kingdom, and their reward will be exactly what they worked for and much, much more!

The possibilities of **your future abode** range from a huge mansion, which will be the headquarters of a city of honor and prestige, to **a humble shack of a servant**. This is the reason the Apostle Paul admonished his converts to "…work out your own salvation with fear and trembling." Phil 2:12

THE COMING KINGDOM WAS THE GREATEST MOTIVATING FORCE IN CHURCH GROWTH

Forty Days Of Intense Training

When Jesus arose from the dead, He used the saturating principle to train and motivate His apostles – "…being seen of them forty days, and speaking of the things pertaining to the kingdom of God." Acts 1:3

Jesus only had forty days to inspire and train the apostles so they would get the Gospel to every person in their generation.

How Could He Do It?

He needed to major on principles that were simple and would capture their minds to fearless service for the rest of their lives. May I suggest some of the principles that **He may have pounded into their minds**:

- They were created in God's image and likeness, and through His power

had great potential as His ambassadors. *Gen 1:26*
- Man was originally created to have dominion, or rule, over the earth – **"...and let them have dominion over...." Gen 1:26**
- Just because Adam failed, God's eternal purpose for creating man did not change.
- David restated man's purpose in **Psalms 8:6, "Thou madest him to have dominion over the works of thy hands; thou hast put all things under his feet:"**
- Jesus taught that everyone, who by faith overcame and "...keepeth my works unto the end, to him will I give power [authority] over the nations." Rev 2:26
- He told them that He would return at any time, so to watch at all times for His coming.
- He explained their jobs to them very clearly. They were to be empowered by God's power, and not their own.
- They were to get the Gospel to every person in Jerusalem, Judea, Samaria,

and to the uttermost parts of the world.
- He said that He was sending them out as lambs among wolves, but if they suffered with Him, they would also reign with Him.

Based upon their complete daily effort in getting the Gospel to every creature, they would eat and drink at His table for 1000 years serving as kings over the twelve tribes of Israel in the Millennial Kingdom.

Peter, Paul, and James' Interpretation of Jesus' Teaching Concerning The Kingdom

The apostle Peter, the first pastor of the first church, was able to lead the church to win and then disciple perhaps as many as 300,000 to 500,000 people in a five to seven year period. How did he get these people to forsake all and endure persecution as they worked and served Jesus? I believe the answer to this question is that he

> Peter told them he would personally be a *"partaker of the glory that shall be revealed,"* speaking of the coming Kingdom. Then he told the pastors that they too could *"receive a crown of glory that fadeth not away."*

was able to take their minds off their present problems of life and give them a long range purpose, by teaching them about the soon coming 1000-year Messianic Kingdom.

Future Glory Offered To Pastors

I Peter, Chapter 5, begins with the apostle Peter addressing the elders (pastors). In verse one, Peter told them he would personally be a "...partaker of the glory that shall be revealed," speaking of the coming Kingdom. Then in verse four, he told the pastors that they too could "...receive a crown of glory that fadeth not away." In verse ten, he gave them the steps that were necessary so that the grace of God would enable them to share in Jesus' eternal glory. They would have to:
- Avail themselves to God's grace
- Realize that they were called to share in His glory
- Go through the suffering and trials which would equip them to be mature, strong, and settled leaders

> This abundant entrance is offered to all who will build properly upon their true foundation, Jesus Christ.

- Wait until the Judgment Seat, where they would get their glorified bodies and receive their places of leadership in the Kingdom

No doubt, Pastor Peter schooled his preacher boys and early leaders in **these steps to eternal glory** and future leadership.

The Kingdom and Glory Offered To All

In the next book, the book of II Peter, the great pastor offered this glory to every born again Christian.

Peter's inspired promise is recorded in II Peter 1:11, where he stated, "For so an entrance [into the 1000-year Kingdom] shall be ministered unto you **abundantly** [with great fanfare] into **the everlasting kingdom** of our Lord and Savior Jesus Christ." This abundant entrance is offered to all who will build properly upon their true foundation, Jesus Christ.

In verse five, he admonished believers to add to their faith (personal faith in Christ as their Savior) virtue (good habits or works). Then, in order, he gave them six

> Peter was a perfect example of someone who **lived in the world**, but was **not of the world**. He lived for Jesus and His coming "well done" in the Kingdom to come.

other principles, which they were to add into their Christian life and practices. They are:
- Knowledge (Biblical knowledge)
- Temperance (Self control)
- Patience (Steadfastness)
- Godliness (God-likeness - Piety)
- Brotherly Kindness (to all men)
- Charity (Godly Love)

Peter told the early disciples that if they were zealous in performing these Christ-like works, then they would have tremendous honor and attention bestowed upon them as their King rewards them when they enter into the Kingdom.

He took their minds off this world and onto eternal things. He gave them goals to strive for in pointing them to the Kingdom. He gave them things to work and suffer for in order to achieve eternal rewards and glory.

Peter was a perfect example of someone who **lived in the world**, but was **not of the world**. He lived for Jesus and His coming "well done" in the Kingdom to come.

His teaching on the coming Kingdom must have given the early disciples an understanding of what Christian life and work was all about. They lived their lives in the light of eternity. They understood what the Christian life was. They performed the Christian life and works. And, because of this, **they spread the Gospel** throughout the known world.

The Secret of Paul's Great Ministry

Whereas Peter inspired the first church and led them to saturate the city of Jerusalem with their doctrine (Acts 5:28), there was one man who stood head and shoulders above any other missionary in spreading the Word of God throughout the world. The man? Paul.

Paul Won and Trained Masses

Much of the book of Acts reveals his exploits, while fourteen of the New Testament books reveal his teachings and passion. There have been few men who have had such singleness of purpose and who were so driven by their love and obedience to Christ. Almost everyone in his generation was impacted in some way by this great warrior; through his preaching, his

> Paul comforted the members of the Philippian church by saying that his imprisonment **was for the furtherance** of the Gospel.

pen, or through those he had personally won. In some way, Paul's life touched and influenced his generation.

His greatest accomplishments were in training and motivation. One can examine the great accomplishments of his ministry.

The Church in Ephesus

It was here, within three years, that Paul and his missionary team of ten preachers were able to win and disciple enough Christians so that all in Asia heard the Word of the Lord, both Jews and Greek. Tens of thousands were saved. (Acts 19:10)

His Ministry as a Prisoner in the City of Rome

One of Paul's greatest burdens was to preach to and to win Roman soldiers so they would carry the Gospel, not only home to Roman citizens, but to the vast areas where the Romans ruled. While he was handcuffed to Roman guards as a prisoner, Paul won and discipled hundreds of the choice members of Caesar's guard. The Gospel spread to Caesar's household as well (Phil 4:22), and Paul comforted the members of the Philippian church by saying that his imprisonment **was for the furtherance** of the Gospel. (Phil 1:12)

Although these two accomplishments were more than most men ever accomplish in an entire ministry, neither represent his greatest work through a local church.

The Crowning Jewel of His Ministry

The church that shines like a spotlight in a dark night is the church at Thessalonica. It was one of Paul's shortest missions, **about three or four weeks**, and he testified that he worked night and day while there.

Paul said that this church became an example to all the believers in Macedonia and Achaia. (Thes 1:7) In addition to that, the whole Christian world had heard of this zealous, committed church. (verse 8)

The people of the church had turned from idols to God **to wait (earnestly looking)** for Jesus' return from Heaven. In fact, there are five chapters in the first Epistle to the Thessalonians. All five of them end in reference to the second coming of Christ:

- "...**wait for his Son** from heaven" I Thes 1:10

- "…in the presence of our Lord Jesus Christ **at his coming**" I Thes 2:19
- "**at the coming** of our Lord Jesus Christ" I Thes 3:13
- "…remain unto the **coming of the Lord**" I Thes 4:15
- "…be preserved blameless **unto the coming…**" I Thes 5:23

The second coming of Christ ushers in the 1000-year reign of Christ. The disciples' minds and hearts were fixed on the future coming Kingdom and they were convinced it could and would happen at any time.

In the second chapter, Paul was revealing his love and effort to develop them into dedicated, strong Christians who would walk worthy of the name of Christ.

Paul reminded them that he was gentle among them when they were first saved, **as a nurse to children**. (verse 7)

He also told them that he not only risked his life to get them saved, but would give his life for them because **they were so dear to him**. (verse 8)

He reminded them of his behavior while he worked with them and for them.

His lifestyle was **holy, just, and blameless**. (verses 9 and 10)

In verse 11, he said that he exhorted (encouraged), comforted, and charged them, **as a father** would exhort, comfort, and charge his own children.

Now all of this is tremendous; and no doubt, if these things were the only things Paul did for his converts in Thessalonica, they would have been a good church.

But verse 12 is the key to their greatness. Paul revealed to them and convinced them why he was demanding so much of them. He explained to them, probably over and over again, why he was **working night and day** for their good. He wanted them to walk worthy of God, so they would hear **God's "well done"** at the Judgment.

Paul's exact words for working so hard and suffering so much in order to develop the people of this great church are found in verse 12. He said, **"That ye would walk worthy of God..."**

Then he explained what so few of God's

> They understood that although they were **in the world**, they were **not of the world system**. Their King was coming back, and it could happen at any moment. And then **they would share in His Kingdom and glory**.

children understand. Please note what Paul taught, **which transformed the members** of the Thessalonian church.

"God, who hath called you unto **his kingdom and glory**." They understood that although they were **in the world**, they were **not of the world system**. Their King was coming back, and it could happen at any moment. And then **they would share in His Kingdom and glory**.

Some may question that the preaching was not about the immediate coming of Jesus to establish His personal Kingdom, but that He was using the word "Kingdom" in the general sense of the word. The unsaved Jews who heard Paul preach were so stirred by his teaching that they caused a riot. The mob brought Jason and some of Paul's workers to the authorities and lodged this complaint, "...These that have turned the world upside down are come hither also; Whom Jason hath received: and these all do contrary to the decrees of Caesar, saying that **there is another king, one Jesus**." Acts 17:6-7

Paul was promising every Christian who took a stand and was

> *Hath not God chosen the poor of this world rich in faith, and **heirs of the kingdom which he hath promised to them that love him?***"

winning souls a special place in the soon coming Kingdom. They would serve 1000 years **under King Jesus.**

Paul's hard work, prayers, examples, tears, and teaching paid off as this church became the crown jewel of this humble man's life and ministry.

James, The Third
Pastor of the Church

Add James' testimony to the teaching of these two giants, Peter and Paul, and you will be able to comprehend the zeal and devotion of their converts.

James said, "Hearken, my beloved brethren, Hath not God chosen the poor of this world rich in faith, and **heirs of the kingdom which he hath promised to them that love him?**" James 2:5 "Heirs of the kingdom" wasn't a phrase that James used to give his members a warm and fuzzy feeling. It was the promise that Jesus used often to get the early saints' **minds off of the world** and to motivate them to give their lives in devoted service.

We have seen the teaching on the imminent coming of the Lord and His Kingdom by the three most influential leaders of that day. They had many of their members looking for Jesus to come in their lifetime. Their lives were fully given to meeting their coming King and hearing Him say, "Well done, thou good and faithful servant, enter into the joy of thy Lord."

This conviction, and their total devotion to Christ, led them to evangelize their generation. Now these three spiritual giants are resting in Heaven, waiting for their future positions in **the soon coming Kingdom**.

THE COMMANDS

"But seek ye first the kingdom of God…"
This command, made first to the apostles in Matt 6:33, is an absolute promise to all believers that **He will personally supply all their needs IF** they will seek first His Kingdom and righteousness.

"Thy Kingdom Come"
In *Luke 11:2,* Jesus also commanded the early disciples to pray for his coming Kingdom every day.

"When You Pray Say"
His command to pray everyday is found in the prayer, "Give us day by day our

daily bread." The first item they were to pray for every day was "Thy Kingdom Come." By praying this simple prayer of only sixty-six words every day was the Lord's way of keeping their minds on His coming Kingdom. The purpose for praying was to keep the disciples motivated as zealous Christians.

Everything Rises or Falls on Leadership

Motivating leadership is the key to church growth. What greater motivation is there for pastors than to "seek first the Kingdom of God" and anticipate hearing Jesus say, **"Well done, come and help me rule the earth for 1000 years?"**

Chapter Two
THE SUBJECTS OF THE KINGDOM

CHARACTERISTICS OF THOSE WHO WILL RULE WITH CHRIST

Clearly Taught In The Old Testament

There are many references in the Old Testament that speak of the glorious future Kingdom, which will be established upon the earth. There are many places that speak of the coming peace, the animals,

> When you read the whole chapter, of forty verses with the future Kingdom in mind, it becomes obvious that the Lord is giving the qualifications of those **who will inherit His future Kingdom**.

and the righteous rule of Christ. There are also many facts concerning His coming reign on earth. *Psalm 47* may not be talking about the Millennial Reign, but it establishes that He is King. The passage of scripture that deals with the principle characteristics of those who will rule with Christ on the earth is ***Psalm 37***. There are **at least five different verses** in this chapter with the promise that the faithful **"shall inherit the**

earth." When you read the whole chapter, of forty verses with the future Kingdom in mind, it becomes obvious that the Lord is giving the qualifications of those **who will inherit His future Kingdom**.

Don't worry or fret. Today, evil doers are prospering and having their way. *Verse 1* **Don't worry about it.** Their success is only temporary. They will soon be cut down. *Verse 2* All over the earth, evil doers plot against and persecute the righteous. Again God says, "**Don't worry about it.** They will be cut off and destroyed." *Verse 38*

Your day is coming. You are in a world governed by the god of this age and his world system. The devil and his workers are against you. But you are to **walk by faith and demonstrate the grace of God** in your life, so you **will inherit the earth** later.

Listen to the Lord's clear commands and His absolute promises:

Command in *verse 3*: Trust in the Lord and do good.

His Promise: You will dwell in the land and be fed.

Command in *verse 4*: Delight thyself in the Lord.

His Promise: He will give you the desires of your heart.
Command in *verse 5*: Commit thy way unto the Lord.
His Promise: He shall bring it to pass.
Command in *verse 9*: Wait on or do service for the Lord.
His Promise: You shall **inherit the earth**.
Command in *verses 10-11*: Watch the destruction of the lost.
His Promise: The meek (humble) shall **inherit the earth**.
Command in *verses 21-22*: Show mercy and give.
His Promise: You will be blessed and **inherit the earth**.
Command in *verses 27-29*: Depart from evil and do good.
His Promise: The righteous (those living righteously) shall **inherit the earth**.

> Depart from evil and do good. The righteous (those living righteously) shall **inherit the earth**.

Command in *verse 34*: Wait (serve) and keep his way.
His Promise: He shall exalt thee to **inherit the earth**.

Studying these verses will shows the characteristics of those who will inherit and

have a place in ruling the earth during the coming kingdom. They are:
- faithful (trusting)
- patient (enduring)
- righteous (living right)
- humble (depending on the Lord)
- waiting on (serving) the Lord
- committed (to righteous principles)
- delighting themselves (in His service)
- strong (in the Lord)

From these verses and other references, it becomes apparent that in order to **have a position of rulership** or inheritance, one must be a practicing Christian who has **a humble nature to do God's will**. The ones whose lives are out of harmony with the world system will have conflict with the world in this age, but if they overcome these conflicts by faith, they **will be leaders in the coming age**.

Confirmation From The New Testament

There are many promises and references of the future Kingdom found in the Old Testament for those who will reign with Christ. These same promises and principles are taught and confirmed in the New Testament.

The Principles That Jesus Gave Guarantee a Ruling Position in His Kingdom

Just as God gave the Ten Commandments to Moses to serve as the foundation of a moral society, Jesus gave eight characteristics of people who will make up the moral foundation and the ruling element in His Millennial Kingdom. Each of these promises was introduced by Jesus in His "Sermon on the Mount." *(Matt 5:3-10)* Each of the promises begins with the word "blessed", which means to be happy. Examine each of these promises in the light of the future kingdom.

> In order to **have a position of rulership**, or inheritance, one must be a practicing Christian who has **a humble nature to do God's will**.

- "Blessed are the poor [humble] in spirit: for theirs is the kingdom of heaven."
- "Blessed are they that mourn [burden for the lost]: for they shall be comforted." (Psalms 126:5-6)

- "Blessed are the meek [submissive to Christ]: for they shall inherit the earth [future]."
- "Blessed are they which do hunger and thirst after righteousness [to know more about Jesus]: for they shall be filled [Paul longed to know Jesus in a more intimate and personal way]." Phil 3:10
- "Blessed are the merciful [a tender heart toward the hurting]: for they shall obtain mercy [be exalted]."
- "Blessed are the pure in heart [right motives]: for they shall see God [comprehend and intimately know Him]."
- "Blessed are the peacemakers: for they shall be called the children [mature, grown up children] of God."
- "Blessed are they which are persecuted for righteousness sake [because of their righteous stand for Christ]: for theirs is the kingdom of heaven [rule on earth]."

Jesus concluded by promising a great reward to **every person who is reviled, persecuted, maliciously maligned, or lied**

about because of his righteous stand for Christ. He knew that:
- those who have a poor or contrite, broken heart
- those who mourn for the lost to be saved
- those who are humbly keeping His commandments
- those who are Bible students, hungry to know and do God's will
- those who are merciful toward a lost and dying world
- those who are pure in heart and who desire what Jesus desired
- those who are peacemakers between Holy God and sinful man
- those who are living righteous lives, which cause people to see their lost condition would be **reviled, persecuted, maliciously maligned, and lied about**.

In *verses 11 and 12*, He gave encouragement to those who were poorly treated by the world as they lived for Christ. He said, "Rejoice and be **exceedingly happy** because your future in the coming

In *II Tim 2:12,* it is clearly stated, "**If we suffer, we shall also reign with him**".

Kingdom has been **greatly enhanced** because of your suffering."

Listen to the very words of Jesus, "Blessed are ye, when men shall revile you, and persecute you, and shall say all manner of evil against you falsely, for my sake. Rejoice, and be exceeding glad: **for great is your reward in heaven**: for so persecuted they the prophets which were before you." Matt 5:11-12

Paul stated in II Tim 3:12, "...all that will live godly in Christ Jesus shall suffer persecution." In II Tim 2:12, it is clearly stated, "If we suffer, we shall also reign with him:..."

The condition of becoming an heir of God and a joint heir with Christ is based on **suffering with Him**. "And if children, then heirs; heirs of God, and joint-heirs with Christ; if so be that we **suffer with him**, that we may be also glorified together." Rom 8:17

CHARACTERISTICS OF THOSE WHO WILL NOT REIGN

Just as there are some verses that give the requirements of those who will have some position in the Millennial Reign, there are also some verses that give the characteristics that **will bring disqualification and judgment**.

JESUS' PLAIN STATEMENT OF TRUTH

Jesus said, "Not every one that saith unto me, Lord, Lord, shall enter into the kingdom of heaven; but he that doeth the will of my Father which is in heaven." Matt 7:21

Please also note in this verse that getting into the Kingdom of God depends on doing the will of God, which means getting to Heaven depends upon one's works. **We know this is not true**, because the Bible clearly declares that one is saved by grace without any works on the part of the person. *(Eph 2:8-9)* Therefore, the truth Jesus is declaring in this verse is that not everyone who states they are saved will have any inheritance in the 1000-year reign, but only those who do the will of God.

THE UNRIGHTEOUS SAVED WILL NOT INHERIT

In *I Cor 6:9a*, Paul asked the question, "Know ye not that the unrighteous **shall not inherit the kingdom of God**?" Then he lists the fleshly practices that will bring disqualification. Those who are living as:

- **Fornicators**
- **Idolaters**
- **Adulterers**
- **Effeminate**
- **Abusers of themselves with mankind**
- **Thieves**
- **Covetous**
- **Drunkards**
- **Revilers**
- **Extortioners**

Paul emphatically stated, "And such were some of you: but ye are washed, but ye are sanctified, but ye are justified in the name of the Lord Jesus, and by the Spirit of our God." I Cor 6:11

> People who go back to that lifestyle **after they are saved will not inherit** the Kingdom of God.

All of the sinners, who fit into one of the above categories, if they are saved, **will have all of their past sins blotted out and stand before God justified**. Justified means they are pure through the righteousness of Christ and stand in His righteousness with **those things blotted out and forgotten**.

When one gets saved, all of his sins are gone. They will not disqualify him from going into the Kingdom. But the principle stated is still true. People who go back to that lifestyle **after they are saved will not inherit** the Kingdom of God.

There are many who carry grace too far. You can never carry grace too far when it pertains to salvation. **It is all of grace.** But grace does not nullify the plain teaching of the Bible about accountability and the Judgment Seat of Christ.

A person could take the verses in *I Cor 6:9-10* and make them stand alone and from those two verses form a doctrine. But one is admonished not to do that. Peter said, "...No prophecy of the scripture is of any private interpretation." II Peter 1:20 This means you cannot take one verse alone to form a doctrine. The Scripture must be interpreted within its setting and must harmonize with the rest of the Bible to be true.

"But fornication, and all uncleanness, or covetousness, let it not be once named among you, **as becometh saints**." Eph 5:3 Here, Paul was clearly speaking about people who have been saved. He said, concerning the saints, "Don't let those sins be once named among you." Then he continued on, "Neither filthiness, nor foolish talking, nor jesting, which are not convenient: but rather giving of thanks." Eph 5:4 Again, it is clear that Paul was talking about **saved people who are doing these things**.

***Verses five through seven* give the punch line.** "For this ye know, that no whoremonger, nor unclean person, nor covetous man, who is an idolater, **hath any inheritance in the kingdom** of Christ and of God." Eph 5:5

Then Paul gives further warning, "Let no man deceive you with vain words: for because of these things cometh the wrath of God **upon the children of disobedience**." Eph 5:6

Paul continued his warning, "Be not **ye** therefore partakers with them." Eph 5:7 It becomes even more emphatic when one remembers that Paul was not writing a general epistle to the world, but to the local church at Ephesus. This church was made up of both practicing and careless members. He was warning the members to be careful of how they live.

Two Fold Nature of the Child Of God

Those that rightly divide the Word of God recognize the teaching that Jesus revealed to Nicodemus in John 3:6, "That which is born of the flesh is flesh; and that which is born of the Spirit is spirit." When a person is saved, he is born of God and **receives a spiritual nature in addition to his fleshly, Adamic nature**.

Paul referred to the works of the flesh in *Gal 5:18-19*, and listed at least seventeen sins of the flesh. In *Gal 5:22-24*, he listed the fruits of the spirit. It is absolutely clear that he was writing to the church at Galatia, which had begun to go into doctrinal error. In *Gal 5:21*, when he finished listing the works of the flesh (speaking to those who had been born again), he strongly warned them saying, "...they which do such things **shall not inherit the kingdom of God**."

The flesh is strong; the devil is the deceiver; and the world is alluring to the child of God. Oh, the pain they will suffer at the Judgment Seat of Christ when they see what their sins have cost them and their families.

> In *Gal 5:21*, when he finished listing the works of the flesh (speaking to those who had been born again), he strongly warned them saying, *"They which do such things **shall not inherit** the kingdom of God."*

***I Cor 6:9-10, Eph 5:3-7, and Gal 5:17-21* teach the same thing.** A person saved by grace has all of those sins gone forever; but after a person is saved by grace, he **cannot** go back to that old lifestyle without severe consequences and forfeiture of rewards. If he does go back he will have no position of rulership in the coming Kingdom.

The question posed is this, "**Where will you live on the other side of the river during the 1000-year reign?**" It is obvious that those who humble themselves and submit themselves, as dedicated servants of Christ, are promised a place of honor and distinction.

It is also stated that one must be careful not to lose the things that "…we have wrought [gained], but receive a full reward." II John 8   A 1000 years is a long time! Where you will live depends on how you respond to the Word of God.

> It is also stated that one must be careful not to lose "the things that they have wrought (gained) but receive a full reward."

Peter, in admonishing Christians who are living in the end times about how they should live, wrote "Wherefore, beloved, seeing that ye look for such things, be diligent that ye may be found of him in peace, without spot and blameless." II Peter 3:14

Chapter Three
OUR GLORIFIED BODIES IN THE KINGDOM

The Bible pointedly says, "...we look for the Savior, the Lord Jesus Christ: who shall change our vile body, that it may be fashioned like unto His glorious body..." Phil 3:20-21

> What a fashion show that will be! In a moment – transformed from the vilest to the most victorious, from the base to the most beautiful, a body like Jesus' glorified, eternal body!

What a fashion show that will be! In a moment – transformed from the vilest to the most victorious, from the base to the most beautiful, a body like Jesus' glorified, eternal body!

SOME THINGS WE KNOW

There are some things recorded in the Bible about the glorified body of Jesus that we can know. These things are a matter of record which is recorded in God's eternal Word.

Jesus Had A Body That One Could See and Recognize

On the Mount of Transfiguration Peter, John, and James beheld the transformation of Jesus from His human body into a spiritual, glorified body. *Matt 17* God caused Moses and Elijah to appear in their glorified bodies with Him. These three men saw and recognized Jesus, Moses, and Elijah although they had never seen the Old Testament saints before. They had no pictures of those renowned men who had been dead for several centuries, but they instantly recognized and knew them.

Paul gave an account of the people who saw Jesus and recognized Him in His glorified body after He was raised from the dead and ministered to them. *I Cor 15:5-8* He also appeared to people personally and to a crowd of over 500. They recognized Him, and most of them gave their lives in spreading the word of His death and resurrection for the remission of sin.

He Wept For Joy

God allowed me to lead a big brute of a man (6'8" tall") to the Lord. He had taken his own thumbs and gouged out his eyes while he was under the influence of narcotics. Big Blind Ben wept uncontrollably when he realized that the first face he would see in his new body would be the blessed face of Jesus. He kept saying, "I will know Him. I will know Him." I put my arm around his big shoulders and said, "Yes, Ben, you will know Him." And, my friend, if you are saved, you will know him too!

Jesus Had a Body That One Could Touch

Some of the most tender scenes in the Bible are when the broken hearted disciples, who had seen their friend and Master brutally crucified right before their very eyes, saw Him in His glorified body.

When Mary asked the two angels, whom she had mistakenly thought were caretakers, "Where hast thou laid him?" From the back came the voice of Jesus who spoke one word, ***"Mary."*** Mary knew that voice and replied, ***"Master."*** (John 20:15-16)

Jesus said, "…Touch me not; for I am not yet ascended to my Father:…" *John 20:17* After His appearance in Heaven as our High Priest, He came back and **the woman embraced His feet**. (Matt 28:9)

The apostles were behind closed, locked doors and suddenly Jesus appeared in their midst. "But they were terrified and affrighted, and supposed that they had seen a spirit." Luke 24:37

And Jesus said unto them, "Behold my hands and my feet, that it is I myself: handle me, and see; for a spirit hath not flesh and bones, as you see me have. And when he had thus spoken, he shewed them his hands and his feet." Luke 24:39-40

> And Jesus said unto them, "Behold my hands and my feet, that it is I myself: handle me, and see; for a spirit hath not flesh and bones, as you see me have.

They were still not fully convinced that He wasn't just a spirit. He asked, "Have ye any meat?" Luke 24:41 When He ate the fish and the honeycomb, they were fully convinced He was alive. Later He told the disciples to reach their hand into His side. From the brief appearances of Jesus before His ascension back to Heaven, we know that He had a body one could recognize; one that ate food and one that you could touch and embrace.

Jesus Had a Body That Had Power Over Matter

Peter and John knew His body had just materialized through the grave clothes when they looked inside the empty tomb. This was the first evidence that gave them hope that Jesus had arisen. Then Jesus appeared to the two disciples on the road to Emmaus. He walked and talked with them and then **He vanished out of their sight.** (Luke 24:13-31)

And as they spoke and told the other disciples about seeing Jesus in His glorified body, He again appeared in their midst. (Luke 24:36)

The dramatic descriptions of John tell it better. "When the doors were shut the disciples were assembled for fear of the Jews, came Jesus and stood in the midst." John 20:19 **Presto! He was gone from one place. Presto!** He appeared in another place even though the doors were locked. Then when His work on earth was finished, He took that unseen elevator back up to Heaven as the apostles stood watching!

> Presto! He was gone from one place. Presto! He appeared in another place even though the doors were locked.

Although He could eat, embrace, and sit at the table with the apostles, He could also materialize right through walls, time, and space and then suddenly appear somewhere else. It almost staggers ones mind to just think about it. Reality and our glorified bodies will soon be ours.

SOME THINGS WE CAN ANTICIPATE

I was baptizing in the Chamah Valley in Mexico. Although it was still morning, the sun was blazing hot. If one accidentally looked into its rays, their vision would be blurred for a few seconds. After baptizing two or three candidates, I would submerge down into the water to my chin. When I stood back up, the very slight wind would cool me off so that I could baptize two or three more people before repeating the process. **The bright, hot sun was dominating!**

Penny and I were traveling to Durango, Colorado and had to cross the Red Mountains, with an elevation of 6500 to 7000 feet above sea level, to get there. The sun was setting just as we climbed the last mountain, and it seemed like we were driving right into **the biggest full moon we have ever seen!** Neither one of us has ever forgotten that breathtaking experience.

Another time, we were at Apache Creek Youth Camp in the extreme western part of New Mexico. Look Out Point is near the top of the mountains there and rises up to 7000 feet in elevation. At night, in that remote area of the country, **it was like the stars were close enough for us to reach up and touch.** Some of the stars were twice or three times larger than their sister stars. It seemed like there were millions upon millions of them, which were twinkling like a choir worshipping their Master.

> When Paul was asked about what type of glorified body the believer would have at the Resurrection, he replied, "Some will have bodies **like the sun!** Some will have bodies **like the moon!** Some will have bodies **like the stars!**"

The Glorified Body of the Believer

When Paul was asked about what type of glorified body the believer would have at the Resurrection, he replied, "Some will have bodies **like the sun!** Some will have bodies **like the moon!** Some will have bodies **like the stars!**"

Some readers may be startled and say, "I never heard that before! Where does it say that in the Bible?"

Paul's exact words were, "But some man will say, **How are the dead raised up?**

and with what body do they come?" I Cor 15:35

Paul answers, "Thou fool, that which thou sowest is not quickened, except it die: And that which thou sowest, thou sowest not that body that shall be, but bare grain, it may chance of wheat, or of some other grain: But **God giveth it a body as it hath pleased him**, and to every seed his own body." I Cor 15:36-38

> *...body that shall be, but bare grain, it may chance of wheat, or of some other grain: But **God giveth it a body as it hath pleased him**, and to every seed his own body."*

We are talking about the future Resurrection in which God will give each believer his own glorified body. The illustration is that one plants a little seed of corn; it dies and comes forth as a beautiful stalk of corn with one or two ears on the stalk.

Paul continues, "All flesh is not the same flesh: but there is one kind of flesh of men, another flesh of beasts, another of fishes, and another of birds." I Cor 15:39

Just as there are differences in the texture and make-up of flesh, there will **be different kinds of glorified bodies**.

In Verses 40 and 41, we come to our illustration. "There are also celestial bodies, and bodies terrestrial: but the glory of the celestial is one, and the glory of terrestrial is another. There is one glory **of the sun**, and another glory **of the moon**, and another glory **of the stars**: for one star differeth from another star in glory."

Now the punch line: "**So also is the resurrection of the dead** [bodies]. It [the body] is sown [like a seed] in corruption; it is raised [like a seed comes up] in incorruption: It [the body] is sown in dishonor [bent over and twisted]; it is raised [like a seed comes up] in glory: it [the body] is sown in weakness [so weak it cannot keep living]; it [the body] is raised in power: It is sown a natural body [designed for a few short years]; it is raised a spiritual body [that will last and shine forever]…" I Cor 15:42-44

This Is In Perfect Harmony

Remember Paul's promise. "Who [Jesus] shall change our vile body, that it may be fashioned like unto his glorious body..." Phil 3:21 When Moses encountered God upon Mount Sinai, he saw only the back side of God as He passed by.

Moses face shown so brightly, they placed a veil over his face when he came down from the encampment. For days, the glow of His countenance was so bright he had to leave his veil on when he talked to people.

When John saw the glorified Christ in Rev 1:17, he said, "...I fell at his feet as dead...." When John described the rapture of the saints who were standing before the throne of Jesus, he said "And he that sat was to look upon **like a jasper and a sardine stone....**" Rev 4:3 Jesus was shining so brightly in His glorified body that John chose two very bright stones in order to try to describe the brightness of His glorified body.

> *Rev 4:3* Jesus was shining so brightly in His glorified body that John chose two very bright stones in order to try and describe the brightness of His glorified body.

So those of His children who are faithful and serve Him acceptably will have bodies that will shine with different shades of brightness forever and ever.

Now it becomes much clearer why the Apostle Paul was still striving and working so hard in his final years. (Phil 3) He not only wanted to shine his very best for the Lord in his earthly life, but he also wanted to shine in his future life beyond the river in the 1000-year reign.

Where Have You Set Your Affections?

Where will you live on the other side of the river? What type of glorified body will you have for all eternity? As an old man, Paul was still working to secure a better resurrection. (Phil 3:13-14) This shows the lifestyle that every older person should adapt as they look forward and prepare to live with Jesus for 1000 years on the other side of the river.

> Where will you live on the other side of the river? What type of glorified body will you have for all eternity?

Chapter Four
LAWS OF PROFIT AND LOSS IN THE KINGDOM

Everything in God's Great Universe is Governed by Laws

Because everything is so precise and orderly, many come to the conclusion was that there must be a super-natural being that created and now maintains this vast universe.

> If he honors all of these laws, he is likely to succeed in farming. If he does not honor them, he will suffer loss and fail.

THERE ARE LAWS WHICH GOVERN PROFIT AND LOSS IN EVERY REALM

The Laws That Govern Profit and Loss in Agriculture

The old farmer honors this law and knows when to plant the seed. In many areas, the window to plant the seed is very narrow. If he plants too early, then a late freeze will damage or destroy the young plants. If he plants his crop too late in the season, rains or winds will come at harvest time, which will greatly damage the harvest. To succeed in farming, he must honor the laws of profit and loss.

The farmer must follow the laws of preparing the soil, of planting the seed, of protecting the crop against its natural enemies and the elements. Then he must harvest the crop and follow the laws of marketing it. If he honors all of these laws, he is likely to succeed in farming. If he does not honor them, he will suffer loss and fail.

The Laws of Profit and Loss in Business

"Profit and loss" is a term that is used frequently in the business and financial world. Charts, graphs, and trends are followed very closely to determine decisions that must be made by the decision makers. Some businesses could not operate without this information, but in everyday business things are much simpler.

> Business success or failure is not left to circumstance. There are laws which, when followed, will bring absolute success. When these laws are violated, the business will fail.

A business that offers a good product, is sensitive to the needs and desires of its customers, and goes the extra mile in customer satisfaction, will more than likely succeed. If a company fails in one of these areas – product, service, or customer satisfaction – it will probably fail.

The Laws of Profit and Loss in Raising a Family

Perhaps the biggest failure in the world is the failure to follow God's laws in raising a family. Our children are the only fruit in the world **that are eternal.** Everything else on this earth is only temporal and will wear out or be burned up some day. To think that God doesn't have laws of profit and loss in raising **children, who are eternal, is unthinkable!**

> These laws are found **in God's manual,** His Holy, eternal Bible.

It is generally accepted in our generation today that raising children to be good, productive, God-fearing citizens is a gamble; that a person cannot be assured that one's children will turn out well. **This thinking violates the laws of profit and loss.** There is no other realm where such explicit laws of profit and loss are given, than in the realm governing the welfare of those He calls "the apple of my eye," who were created in His image and likeness. These laws are found **in God's manual,**

His Holy, eternal Bible.

The problem lies in that most people do not read His instructions. There are many of God's children who do not look at the Bible as God's manual **for raising their children.** Those that do accept the Bible as a manual in raising their children often times pick and choose **the principles they want to teach.** Some may follow the laws as closely as they can, but then nullify much of their training **by outward flaws** in their own lives.

Business success or failure is not left to circumstance. There are laws which, when followed, will help bring success. When these laws are violated, the business will fail.

The world has profited greatly by parents who have followed God's laws of profit and loss in raising their children. The world has been changed and generations blessed by a Godly product of a praying, saintly mother. The real fruition of this foundation will be amplified in the Millennium and eternal age.

The world is in chaos today by the teachings of parents who have followed flawed principles and worldly psychology in raising their children. They not only fail to recognize God's Word as His manual for raising children, but many even fail to recognize God as the Supreme Being.

> If there are laws of profit and loss which dictate the outcome and results in every realm of this life, then you can absolutely expect our eternal God to have laws-of profit and loss in the coming millennial age.

Many of these people and their children, who have violated His laws of profit and loss in their families, suffer shipwreck and destruction. Oh, what tragedies and heartbreak they face as this three score and ten years life ends and they transfer into the eternal age.

If there are laws of profit and loss, which help shape the outcome and results in every realm of this life, then **you can absolutely expect** our eternal God to have laws of profit and loss in the coming Millennial age.

LAWS WHICH GUARANTEE TREMENDOUS REWARDS FOR THOSE THAT HONOR THEM

Jesus Offers Kingship to Some

In the first chapter of Revelation, the Bible declares this truth. In verses five and six it states, "...Unto him? that loved us, and washed us **[loosed** us] from our sins in his own blood, And hath made us **[lifted us]** kings and priests unto God and his Father; to him be glory and dominion for ever and ever. Amen."

Satan takes this tremendous Bible doctrine, which was given to motivate men to look beyond this life, and corrupts it.

The devil does this by raising up a cult who put their own spin about being a god over their own kingdom, which will be populated by their children, who will be produced by his many wives and descendants. The devil knew that as this false religion grew, much teaching would have to be done by the true churches in order to refute this false doctrine. The refuting of their falsehood would have the effect of blinding men to the true teaching that some men would serve as kings in the Millennium.

In refuting error, many times efforts are made to show what is false. They may do a good job of doing that, but they fail to show what the truth is concerning the doctrine.

"…have thou authority over ten cities." the Bible states in Luke 19:17. In Matthew, Jesus promised, "…thou hast been faithful over a few things, I will make thee ruler over many things...." Matt 25:21. And in Rev 2:27, Jesus said to the overcomers that He would give them **power (authority) over the nations.** His words were, "And he shall rule them with a rod of iron...."

The King of Kings promised the overcomers, in Rev 2:25-26, that they would sit with Him on His throne and, together, they would rule the world.

This is the positive teaching of the coming Kingdom. Most people's minds are blinded by the teaching they have heard in refuting the devil's false propaganda about the Kingdom.

WHY OFFER THESE TREMENDOUS POSITIONS OF REWARD AND HONOR?

The question that comes into the minds of some is, "Why would Jesus offer such tremendous positions of honor to His people after all He has already done for them?" He suffered and died on the cross;

> The King of Kings promised the over comers, *in Rev 2:25-26,* that they would sit with Him on His throne and, together, they would rule the world.

and through that sacrifice, believers have eternal life, a future glorified body, and a home in Heaven. After all that He has done for us by His grace and love, why would He offer these further rewards?

REASONS FOR THESE FUTURE REWARDS AND POSITIONS OF HONOR IN THE KINGDOM

Positions of Glory Offered in Order to Teach Man to Strive for Things That are Eternal

One of the first commandments Jesus gave in His early ministry to mankind was, "Lay not up for yourselves treasures on this earth, where you will lose them during your lifetime or leave them when you die. But lay up for yourselves **treasures** in Heaven, where they will be safe and preserved for you." Matt 6:19-20

> Satan takes this tremendous Bible doctrine, which was given to motivate men to look beyond this life, and corrupts it

This command seems to have fallen on deaf ears, as man runs recklessly about this earth to **get all that he can.** In order to help man see that **he is eternal** and that this short span on earth, called life, is so brief and uncertain, God **offers rich and tremendous rewards** to those who find and fulfill their purpose. These rewards are promised to all that will listen to the Bible, realize they are eternal beings, find their place on this earth as a steward of Christ, and pursue their purpose, which is to be an ambassador for Christ. Jesus offered them a rich pay check for doing this.

These rewards are so much more than what the world offers, and **they are eternal.** By offering these rewards, God is striving to **get man to work for Him and** not waste his life following after things of the world that will perish.

Positions of glory offered in order to fulfill man's desire for greatness. Man, by nature, wants to triumph and **"be somebody."** Every little boy wants to grow up and be some kind of "star." God created man to **have dominion over this earth.** Man has an innate desire to excel and do great things. After a few years, most people are beaten down by the world and the devil and **succumb** to a mediocre life and existence

God offers these great and glorious positions in order to capture man's inner desires and propel him to greatness. He uses the example of the first generation of Christians, **who were fisherman, common laborers, and housewives,** in order to try to get them to see that they too, **by the grace and mercy of God,** can do great things. He holds out the carrot of future positions in the Millennium in order to motivate them to throw themselves into the **spiritual realm of life.** To satisfy their desire for greatness, God offers a simple way for the average man to excel and become "somebody" in the age to come.

Positions of glory offered to man in order to offset what the devil and the world offer. The devil and the world are **bidding** for the lives and souls of man. They are doing everything in their power to entice, capture, and then destroy mankind. What do they offer for the souls and lives of their victims? **They offer them the world!** They promise to make them **top dog with power, prestige, and lordship over others.** They promise them pleasure, good times, plenty of adoration, and recognition from peers and subordinates. The appeal and distraction comes from every side. **Man's hunger for popularity** and fame makes him an easy victim for the devil to trap, and eventual destroy.

The devil even tried this allurement on Jesus in the wilderness, where he promised, "Worship me and I will give you the kingdom and power."

Jesus offers positions of glory and honor in order to **out-trump the devil's offer,** and get man to set his affection on eternal greatness. God surpasses the allurement of the devil by promising real and lasting fulfillment in the coming Kingdom, which outshines anything the devil can offer – ruler over many things or a kingship for 1000 years.

Positions of glory offered to reveal Jesus' great heart and nature to honor and bless His people. Jesus' nature dictates that He share His blessings with those He loves. When He offers lasting and prestigious rewards, it reveals His loving and giving nature. It is just a part of Him to do so, because **God is love.** Love honors and shares. Love is the opposite of selfishness, and is fulfilled in giving and sharing.

Jesus offers great and lasting rewards with positions of honor and distinction **because it blesses and fulfills His nature to do so.**

Positions of glory offered in order to take the promise out of the abstract and place it into the concrete. The word "abstract" comes from two words: "ab," which means from, and "stract," which means to draw. Together they mean "thoughts apart from any particular instance or material." When one speaks in an abstract way, they are stating a principle and not talking about any particular instance.

The word "concrete" comes from two words also: "con," meaning together, and "crete," which means to grow. Together, the two words mean "formed into a solid mass."

Many times we make the promises of God abstract that a person cannot see. When we say that positions of glory should be taken out of the abstract and made concrete; we want to show the person the absolute promise and not the vague promise. For example:

Jesus said, "If you will serve me faithfully, I will bless you," **that is abstract**.

Jesus said, "If you will serve me faithfully, I will make you ruler over five cities," **that is concrete**.

Jesus said, "If you serve me faithfillly, I will reward you," **that is abstract**.

Jesus said, "If you serve me faithfully, I will let you eat and drink at my table for 1000 years," **that is concrete**.

Jesus said, "If you will give up your all and follow me, I will bless you," **that is abstract.**

When Jesus said, "If you will give up your all and follow me, I will reward you 100 fold (10,000 times your investment)," **that is concrete.**

Man can understand the concrete promise and, with faith, work toward it regardless of his problems or personal feelings. But a man who has an abstract promise such as, "I will bless you," may lose sight of it in times of trouble and confusion.

> God offers great and wonderful concrete promises in order to secure and keep a person's attention while lie works toward the sure promises of God.

Jesus knew that nature of man. We are like little children. In fact, He calls us little children on many occasions. If you promise a little child an ice cream cone providing he is a good boy, then he will expect an ice cream cone and will pester you until he gets it.

God offers great and wonderful **concrete promises** in order to secure and keep a person's attention while he works toward the sure promises of God. We, in this generation, need to take God's promises out of the abstract and make them **very clear and concrete.**

But, just as there are profits in the coming kingdom, there are principles which bring chastisement and loss. Please consider the following principles.

LAWS WHICH ARE VIOLATED BRING HEARTBREAK, TEARS, AND LOSS IN THE KINGDOM

Now, the author is aware that this section will cut against the grain of some of God's greatest preachers and scholars. But

> LAWS WHICH ARE VIOLATED BRING HEARTBREAK, TEARS, AND LOSS IN THE KINGDOM.

please, before you judge too harshly or judge this as some kind of "Baptist purgatory," reason with me a little.

We know there will be different degrees of rewards during the millennium.

We know there are going to be different degrees of punishment in hell.

Every Bible teacher I know accepts and believes those two statements. But for some reason, it is difficult to believe or accept that the child of God who becomes an enemy of Jesus Christ should have any repercussion or chastisement for the entire 1000-year period. Somehow or another, in their reasoning, that violates grace. My answer is that there has always been a time of grace, followed by judgment.

Grace Followed by Judgment

God offered a choice to Pharaoh, and he refused and hardened his heart. God offered his grace again and again to Pharaoh, and each time he hardened his heart. Finally, after offers of grace, God hardened Pharaoh's heart and judgment came.

The Law of the Sabbath

The Jews were not only supposed to cease work on the seventh day, but they were to let the land have rest and refurbish itself every seven years.

Every seventh day, the Jews were to spend the whole day away from their labors.

They were to teach their children as they dedicated the whole day to worship and honor God as the Lord, Creator, and Savior.

God also had a law of the Sabbath year for the land, every seventh year. If the Jews had honored the law of the weekly Sabbath day, they would have been able to, by faith, obey God and allow the land to rest so the poor could benefit from its production:
- The Jews refused to obey
- The Jews became carnal
- The Jews then became backslidden

The process was followed by the chastisement of God. After several years of chastisement, God took them out of their land and sold them into slavery. This allowed the land to have rest for seventy years. II Chronicles 36:20-21 Seventy years is actually a short period of time - the average length of a man's life - but it illustrates grace before judgment.

> After several years of chastisement, God took them out of their land and sold them into slavery. This allowed the land to have rest for 70 years

BLINDNESS CAME OVER ISRAEL AS A NATION

Grace Offered in the Wilderness

Again, we have grace offered to Israel as He brought them out of Egypt. Grace was rejected again and again; then the judgment of forty years wandering in the wilderness.

Grace Offered in the Land of Promise

Grace continued to be offered under the leadership of Joshua, but the Jews backslid again and again. Each time God chastised them and offered grace again. Finally, the judgment came and their kingdom was divided.

Grace Offered to the Kings

Grace was offered over and over and over again to the kings. Finally judgment came and the Jews lost their freedom and their land and were scattered throughout the world.

The Big Question

The apostles asked Jesus, "Why do you speak to them (Jews) in parables? Matthew 13:10

Jesus answered the apostles' question by saying, "...Because it is given unto you to know the mysteries of the kingdom of heaven, **but to them it is not given.**" Matthew 13:11

"Why is this Jesus? Why wasn't it given unto the Jews to understand?"

Jesus answered, "For whosoever hath, to him shall be given, and he shall have more abundance: but whosoever hath not, from him shall be taken away even that he hath. Therefore speak I to them in parables: because they seeing see not; and hearing they hear not, neither do they understand." Matthew 13:12-13

Jesus is saying, "I worked with them through the prophets, through wars, through chastisement. I have tried to help them in every way possible!"

In verse 14, Jesus speaks about the prophet's prophecy. **In essence, they (the Jews) don't want to hear.** They don't want to see. They don't want to understand. Because of this continual offer of grace and their refusal, He

> Because of this continual offer of grace and their refusal, He will not let them, as a nation; spurn the grace of God again. They will suffer the consequences of their past decisions.

would not let them, as a nation; **spurn the grace of God again**. They will suffer the consequences of their past decisions. Notice the truth of this principle which is stated in II Chronicles 36:16, "But they mocked the messengers of God, and despised his words, and misused his prophets, until the wrath of the LORD arose against his people, till there was no remedy."

Now Answer This Question

For two to three thousand years, God has basically left the Jewish nation spiritually blind. They rejected every offer of grace and, as a nation, have paid the horrible price ever since. This judgment has lasted for a much longer time than 1000 years.

Was God too harsh in His judgment? Absolutely not! He saw that His grace, love, and working with them was rejected and they would not turn to Him. Because of this, they must bear the consequence of rejecting His love and mercy. The consequence is judgment.

> They willfully made bad decisions again and again and again. Finally, their loving Savior said, "Son, **I'll see you at the Judgment Seat."**

God Has Done the Same Thing For Us

Every one of God's children who have made shipwrecks of their lives, have done so after God's grace was rejected. God worked with them and offered grace. They would not listen and turned away. They neglected His offer of mercy. They willfully made bad decisions again and again. Finally, their loving Savior said, "Son**, I'll see you at the Judgment Seat."**

If the Jewish nation had to bear their punishment for refusing God's grace, not once, not twice, not three times, but over and over again? If they had to suffer for several hundreds of years. Then why is there a problem with individuals who have done the same thing, **living with the fruits of their deeds for the 1000-year reign?**

It Will all End Before an Eternal Heaven

At the end of the 1000 years, the Great White Throne Judgment for the lost will take place.

> Do you mean the sinner suffers eternally and the ones who hindered them from being saved don't have any consequences?

The lost will be cast into the Lake of Fire forever. Is God cruel? Absolutely not!

He did everything in His power to turn every sinner to Jesus and give them eternal life. Because they are eternal beings, they must be placed somewhere. They made the choice of where they will spend eternity **by rejecting God's offer of grace.**

One of God's biggest obstacles to overcome in saving sinners – one of the biggest hindrances to His effort of saving the lost – **is His backslidden children.**

Do you mean the sinner suffers eternally and the ones who hindered them from being saved don't have any consequences?

God's Mercy Intervenes

The wayward child will only have to endure his pain for a short time – as the eternal God counts time and in comparison to what the lost will suffer.

After the Great White Throne Judgment, God will create a new Heaven and a new earth. At that point, He will gather His big family together and put His loving arm around the disobedient child and say, "Son, you have suffered enough."

He will wipe the tears from his eyes. He will wipe the memory from his mind and "the former things are passed away." *Rev 21:4*

Judgment Without Mercy

God will not change His Word just because we live in an age that wants to depend too much on the grace and mercy of a loving Father. The Word of God IS the Word of God and every believer will be judged by it as they stand before the Judgment Seat of Christ. There are some laws that are eternal and they will be applicable at the Judgment Seat. James warned that, "For he shall have judgment without mercy, that hath shewed no mercy...." James 2:13

This followed a long discourse that warned against the vainness of lip service, and warned against loving in thought and in word only; and concluded that faith without works, or failing to help solve a need when we can, is no faith at all. He termed it "dead faith." There are many people who are good Christians in their mind and they know how to talk a good talk, but they are absolutely facing the millennial position that will bring them many tears.

THREE ETERNAL, UNCHANGING LAWS

Let us examine three eternal laws which will come to full fruition in the coming 1000-year Kingdom.

The Law of Sowing and Reaping

One of the most Joyful scriptures for the faithful Christian is, "...Blessed are the dead which die in the Lord from henceforth: Yea, saith the Spirit, that they may rest from their labours; **and their works do follow them.**" Rev 14:13 If this is true for the faithful servants, **it is true for the unfaithful servants as well.**

> A backslidden Christian dies and his woes compound, as the works that he put into motion during his lifetime keep on following him.

Paul warned that a person should not be deceived. Then he said, "...God is not mocked: for whatsoever a man soweth, that shall he also reap. For he [speaking to Christians] that soweth to his flesh shall of the flesh reap corruption...." Gal 6:7-8

A backslidden Christian dies and his woes compound, as the works that he put into motion during his lifetime keep on following him.

Backslidden Lot is a perfect example of a Christian who pitched his tent toward Sodom (the world and its monetary benefits) and enjoyed success for a little while. Then all of his lofty goals vanished and the castle he had built in his mind came crumbling down. In disgrace, he died a lonely old man, the father of Moab and Ammon. Lot was saved, but the millions of descendants of Moab and Amnion were entrenched in false religion and false hope. For 1000 years, Lot will remember and face the consequences of his misspent, backslidden life.

> For 1000 years, Lot will remember and face the consequences of his misspent, backslidden life.

The law of sowing and reaping will not be suspended by grace. "He shall have Judgment without mercy to him who showed no mercy." David said that God would "...renderest to every man according to his work." Psalms 62:12

> All of the seeds that have been sown, **both good and bad,** will keep working until the Judgment Seat.

All of the seeds that have been sown, **both good and bad,** will keep working until the Judgment Seat. Those that sowed to the flesh will find the same end as did Esau, who sought repentance with tears but found none.

The Law of Whosoever Exalteth Himself Shall be Abased

Pride is man's characteristics that **God hates the most.** Peter warned preachers that "...God resisteth the proud, and giveth grace to the humble." I Peter 5:5

> Jesus preached, "For whosoever exalteth himself shall be abased; and he that humbleth himself shall be exalted."

God vividly demonstrated to the world what He would do to those who lifted themselves up in pride when He humbled Nebuchadnezzar, the first world ruler. Daniel 4:1-37

He humbled the highest monarch on earth and made him live **like a beast for seven years to demonstrate the judgment God will execute toward those who are proud.**

> Just as the results of the lives of the faithful will be reflected in the positions they have in triumph during the entire 1000 years, so will the unfaithful have to suffer the consequences of tears, shame and **regret for the entire 1000 years.**

Jesus preached, "For whosoever exalteth himself

shall be abased; and he that humbleth himself shall be exalted." Luke 14:11

God told Israel through Isaiah the prophet, "The lofty looks of man shall be humbled, and the haughtiness of men shall be bowed down, and the LORD alone shall be exalted in that day. For the day of the Lord of hosts shall be upon every one that is proud and lofty, and upon every one that is lifted up; and he shall be brought low." Isaiah 2:11-12

The day the Lord is referring to is the **Day of Judgment.** The Christians who were too proud to submit to the drawing of the Holy Spirit and repent to make things right, **will be brought low and their tears will flow.**

> Many of God's people have developed a **holier-than-thou attitude** toward other people, **which has repelled sinners from the Gospel.**

Just as the results of the lives of the faithful will be reflected in the positions they have in triumph during the entire 1000 years, so will the unfaithful have to suffer the consequences of tears, shame, and **regret for the entire 1000 years.**

The Law of Judging and Being Judged

This law is very close to the law of reaping what you sow, **the difference is in attitude.** Jesus said, "Judge not." Why? He goes ahead to explain why a person should not be critical and judgmental. It will bring judgment back to that person. Many of God's people have developed a **holier-than-thou attitude** toward other people, **which has repelled sinners from the Gospel** instead of drawing them to the Lord. They will face that religious attitude at the Judgment Seat of Christ.

> If a person doesn't obey the command of **sowing the message of salvation in tears** as he seeks sinners on this earth, **he will shed tears** over his misspent life at the Judgment Seat.

Other Christians' favorite verse seems to be, "by this shall all men know that you are my disciples **that you go around straightening everybody out."** This rendition of the verse **wounds people** instead of wooing them to Jesus. The verse actually states, "By this shall all men know that ye are my disciples, if ye have **love** one to another." John 13:35

Perpetuating religious standards and traditions, and judging those that fall short was not the purpose of Jesus Christ on this earth. He came to seek and to save sinners. These judgmental and critical attitudes must be replaced with a humble and loving spirit toward the lost. If a person doesn't obey the command of **sowing the message of salvation in tears** as he seeks sinners on this earth, **he will shed tears** over his misspent life at the Judgment Seat.

The Eternal Laws of God Will Carry Over To the Next Age

If one has sown to the flesh in this age, **he will live with the horrible crop** his seeds produce in the next age.

If one has been proud and haughty in this life, he will be humbled and abased in his new position of tears in the next age.

If one has been judgmental and critical serving his religion in this life, he will serve under the same spirit as the recipients of those seeds sown for the coming 1000-year reign.

> The laws of profit and loss dictate that both of these conditions will be found in the Kingdom.

Just as many of God's children will bask in the glory of God during the 1000-year reign for their faithful service, so will many of his unfaithful children be living with pain and tears because of their backslidden and careless life. The laws of profit and loss dictate that both of these conditions will be found in the Kingdom.

The personal question that you should dwell upon is, "Where will you live on the other side of the river?" What kind of crop will you be blessed with or cursed by for 1000 years? Whatever you sow in this life will likely multiply 1000 times in your life during the 1000 years.

Please Take Heart

Many of God's people will realize for the first time why God expects and commands them to live **a dedicated life of service.** If Jesus came today, they would be totally unprepared and ashamed. Much of their life's works would be judged and burned at the Judgment Seat of Christ.

To the dear people who have wasted much of their lives and read this book the author has a word of **hope and encouragement.** Before you finish this book, you will see the gracious offer that Jesus has made so that you can be greatly

> There is a big house and a place of leadership waiting for you to claim. Your life is not over yet.

rewarded and honored on the other side of the river. There is a big house and a place of leadership waiting for you to claim. Your life is not over yet. Although you have not been a faithful, dedicated Christian who is getting people saved, your loving Father has a way for you to change all of that before you cross over in death or He comes for you. So take heart, the best (for you) is yet to come.

Chapter Five
THOSE WHO WILL BE TRANSFERRED INTO THE KINGDOM

There are some things we can know about our eternal glorified bodies. We may not comprehend everything, but we can know them. Then there are some things we can anticipate. They may seem to be from a science fiction story, but they are not. Our future bodies are something our Father has designed for us. Again, it may be beyond our wildest imagination, but we can look forward with great anticipation to our future, eternal bodies.

In this and the following four chapters, we will begin to study the various people who will make up the population of the Kingdom. There will be three different categories of people who will make up the population of this coming Kingdom:
- There are people who will transfer into the Kingdom.
- There will be people who will triumph in the Kingdom.
- There will be people who will shed tears in the Kingdom.

THE PEOPLE WHO WILL BE TRANSFERRED INTO THE KINGDOM

In the Kingdom to come, there will be at least two types of citizens. In addition to those in their new, glorified, eternal bodies, **there will be people in their natural bodies.**

In the Old Testament, there are different nations mentioned that will exist during the 1000-year reign. In Matthew 25:31-46, we have an account of the judgment of those nations. Please note that this judgment takes place after the Tribulation period when Jesus comes back to the earth as King. Matt 25:31

- There are people who will transfer into the Kingdom.
- There will be people who will triumph in the Kingdom.
- There will be people who will shed tears in the Kingdom.

The criteria upon which He will judge the nations will be based on how they treated the Jewish and Christian people. If the people of a nation treated Jews and Christians kindly and with tolerance, they will be judged a **sheep nation**. The nations who discriminated against and persecuted them will be judged **as a goat nation**.

Jesus will call all nations before Him and place the sheep nations on His right hand and the goat nations on His left. (verses 32 and 33)

> Jesus will call all nations before Him and place the sheep nations on His right hand and the goat nations on His left.

The nations will be rewarded or punished in direct response to how they treated Christians and His chosen nation, Israel. (verses 42 through 46)

In Matt 25:36, Jesus said, "I was sick, and ye visited me." In verses 37 through 39, the people that make up the sheep nations will ask, "When did we see you sick and visited you?" Jesus answers in verse 40, "Inasmuch as ye have done it unto one of the least of these my brethren, ye have done it unto me."

After He commends them and invites them to enter into the Kingdom, He turns and repeats to those who make up the goat nations - who were cold and unkind to His people (Jews and Christians) - "Depart from me, ye cursed, into everlasting fire." (verse 41)

Jesus will instantly cast the people who make up the goat nations into everlasting fire. (Matt 25:41) Then He will say to the sheep nations, "Come, ye blessed of my Father, inherit the kingdom prepared for you from the foundation of the world." Matt 25: 34

> The nations will be rewarded or punished in direct response to how they treated Christians and His chosen nation, Israel.

The people of the sheep nations, **who survive the Great Tribulation Period,** will be transferred over into the Millennial Reign in their natural bodies. **They will not be raptured**. None of them will come up from the grave. They were able, with the help of the Lord, to have lived through the worst time the world has ever seen. In their natural, human bodies, Jesus will transfer them over from the judgment of the nations and they will continue to live in their natural bodies

> The people of the sheep nations, **who survive the Great Tribulation Period,** will be transferred over into the Millennial Reign in their natural bodies.

in the place He has prepared for them in the 1000-year reign. There will be millions of these people **who go into the Millennial Reign in their natural bodies.**

In the Millennial Reign of Christ, these people from the sheep nations who have survived the tribulation period with their physical lives will be the subjects of the Kingdom **who will be ruled over.** The Lord Jesus and those He

> **The sucking child.** "The sucking child (or baby) will play on the hole of the asp "(Isaiah 11: 8) indicates that there will be babies born during this peaceful reign.

has chosen to rule with Him will show the world how God intended Adam and his vast numbers of children to live on earth - **in peace and harmony with each other and with the elements of the earth.** The tempter (Satan) will be in the Bottomless Pit for 1000 years. Therefore the people of the earth will be at peace with one another.

Population Growth for One Thousand Years

Please note the different ages of this growing and expanding race in their natural bodies.

The sucking child. "...the sucking child [or baby] will play on the hole of the asp...." (Isaiah 11:8) indicates that there will be babies born during this peaceful reign.

The weaned child. This larger child who is walking and eating table food, "...shall put his hand on the cockatrice den." Isaiah 11: 8

A little child. This primarily refers to junior age children who will pet a lion, or perhaps a leopard, and will play with him. Isaiah 11: 6

There will be no fear or threat from any animal as the children freely play with them as pets.

These three statements indicate that there will be no death among the ages, which have a high mortality rate in much of the world today. What a relief to mothers and what fun it must be for the kids not to have the pain and fear that terrify many children today.

God's Purpose Finally Fulfilled

Although Adam and his family completely blew it and made the earth a place of death, rebellion, and destruction, God will finally enjoy His pleasure and will for man on this earth.

> God's Word declares, "a little one shall become a thousand, and a small one a strong nation ".

Adam yielded the lordship of the earth to the devil. But the devil violated that lordship, and King Jesus will put him in the bottomless pit for 1000 years and establish the reign that He first intended Adam and his family to enjoy.

In keeping with the different ages of young children, God's Word declares, "A little one shall become a thousand, and a small one a strong nation...." Then God affirms that He, the Lord, "...will hasten it [bring it to pass] in His time." Isaiah 60:22

In the previous verse God declares, "Thy people also shall be all righteous: they shall inherit the land, for ever, the branch of my planting, the work of my hands, that I may be glorified." Isaiah 60:21 Jesus will get the glory from the way people live during that time.

He has already stated **the beauty of the trees** (verse 13), **the wealth of the land** (verse 17), **the peace the land enjoys** (verse 18), and that He will be their glory as well as the light of the land (verse 19) for the benefit of His people. He is dwelling with them with the intent of making them happy.

Isaiah promises that God will:
- "...comfort all that mourn."
- "...give unto them beauty for ashes,"
- "the **oil** of joy for the mourning,"
- "the **garment** of praise for the spirit of heaviness...."

His people **will "...be called trees of righteousness, the planting of the Lord...."** Why? "...that he [God] might be glorified." Isaiah 61:2-3

> God will:
> - "... comfort all that mourn."
> - ..."give unto them beauty for ashes"
> - "the **oil** of joy for the mourning"
> - "the **garment** of praise for the spirit of heaviness...."

Again, we see God receiving glory as He cares for and ministers to the people of the earth. They will enjoy the fruits of the labor as they:

- "...build the old wastes...."
- "...raise up the former desolations...."
- "...repair the waste cities, the desolation of many generations" (verse 4)

The result of His effort, with a peaceful people, is tremendous growth and development. As stated in the descriptive verse, "the desert will blossom like a rose."

> These are descriptions of revival and spiritual growth. Everything on earth is exciting under His loving leadership and blessings.

They will be served as they work as the ministers of God. Please note these different servants and workers who will serve

during the Kingdom:
- "...strangers shall stand and feed your flocks...."
- "...sons of the alien shall be your plowmen and your vinedressers."
- "...ye shall eat the riches of the Gentiles...."
- "...in their glory shall ye boast yourselves." (verses 5 and 6)
- "...God will cause righteousness and praise to spring forth before all the nations." (verses 11)

The people will greatly rejoice in the Lord, and God will clothe them with the garments of salvation. They will be covered with the robes of righteousness. They will be decked out with ornaments as a bridegroom. They will be adorned like a bride with jewels.

These are descriptions of revival and spiritual growth. Everything on earth is exciting under His loving leadership and blessings.

PERFECT PEACE ON EARTH

The implements of war will be transformed into plows and farm equipment.

> What a day that will be when the people of the earth dwell together with nothing to fear or be anxious about!

"They shall beat their swords into plowshares, and their spears into pruning hooks: nation shall not lift up sword against nation, neither shall they learn war anymore." Isaiah 2:4

No military, no training, no wars; just peace and righteousness under a righteous and loving Lord. What a contrast between King Jesus and the present day administrators who are running things in the world today.

> All news will be good news. People's minds will not be oppressed by the reports of tragedies, death, or destruction.

What a day that will be when the people of the earth dwell together with nothing to fear or be anxious about!

A LAND FILLED WITH GOOD NEWS

In America, the liberal press and the broadcast news media feature bad news. This is especially true if the news places God and fundamental Christians in a bad or shameful light. One of the most notable changes during the 1000-year reign will be the positive, edifying news under the rule of King Jesus.

Isaiah speaks of that glorious day. He says, "They shall not hurt nor destroy in all my holy mountain [government]: for the earth shall be full of the knowledge of the Lord, as the waters cover the sea." Isaiah 1:9

All news will be good news. People's minds will not be oppressed by the reports of tragedies, death, or destruction.

The people, in their natural bodies, will learn about God and enjoy the fruition of peace (at last) on earth.

A SURPRISING THING

Even in the beautiful land of utopia and peace, not all of the people who reach the age of accountability will accept Jesus as their Savior, and be saved. (Isaiah 65:20)

This will be basically true because people will still have the freedom of choice as they live in a body that still has a depraved, carnal mind, and a rebellious nature.

By the end of the 1000 years, no doubt the vast majority of the people in their natural bodies will be saved. However, there will be quite a number that will still be lost, in spite of the presence of the Lord and the just and fair way of life. Rev 20:9

In this chapter, it has been established that sinners will live on this earth in their natural bodies during the 1000-year reign. God will show His will for the human race to live on a perfect earth as a big happy family. He will also show that **the devil is the true villain** and not God. Under the devil's administration for 6000 years, there has been **nothing but death and destruction.**

Under the administration of King Jesus, there will be no death and destruction. As soon as Jesus lets the devil out of hell for a short time, there will be war, crime, and destruction once again. The God who is blamed for all of earth's problems **will be exonerated and the true villain exposed**. Jesus will be revealed to the world as a loving Savior, while the devil will be exposed as the destroyer of man. The Millennium will close with the monster and destroyer of hopes and dreams cast into hell forever. A brighter chapter will then open for God's family, **as we enter into the eternal age.**

In the next chapter, we will see how Jesus' honors and rewards His people who denied themselves the personal things they wanted to do in order to obey Christ. We will see the ones He rewards and the lives they lived that qualified and elevated them to receive the level of living in the "big house" as they reign for the complete 1000 years.

> He will also show that **the devil is the true villain** and not God. Under the devil's administration for 6000 years, there has been **nothing but death and destruction.**

WHERE WILL YOU LIVE?

In the coming dispensation of peace, honor, righteousness, and prosperity, **where will you live**? Have you worked for prestige and prosperity in this short life on this side of the river, at the expense of forfeiting your mansion and glory on the other side of the river?

The coming reign of Christ will be the most exciting time that the world has ever known. God designed man to have dominion

> In the coming dispensation of peace, honor, righteousness, and prosperity, **where will you live**?

over the earth. Will you be part of **those that will rule and reign with Christ**, or will you have sabotaged your chances of reigning by living **for your own good and gain on this side of the river?**

Chapter Six
ETERNAL LIFE IS A GIFT, REWARDS ARE EARNED

Some foundational truths will be established before we discuss the great rewards which are given in the next chapter.

WHY DOES GOD OFFER REWARDS?

One may ask, "Why would God offer rewards after all that he has already done for the child of God?"

God is a giver. There are two types of people in the world, takers and givers. God is a giver and his nature is most fulfilled when he gives. He gives all mankind life, air, strength, and ability to move and enjoy living. He has given each of his children eternal life. He has designed a life that is good, acceptable, and perfect for each of his children if they will only submit to his leading. **His nature is to give**.

> **God is a giver.** There are two types of people in the world, takers and givers. God is a giver and his nature is most fulfilled when he gives.

God is a sharer. Every parent will confess that the greatest fulfillment and happiness they receive is when they share their love and substance with their loved ones (especially with their children). We received that nature from our Heavenly Father, who also receives his greatest gratification in sharing.

It will help one to understand the doctrine of salvation and rewards when he sees that there are **three great differences between** the two doctrines.

First, salvation is a free gift (Romans 6:23), while a reward must be earned (I Corinthians 3:8).

Second, a child of God has eternal life now (I John 5:11-13), while rewards must be earned and will be passed out at the Judgment Seat of Christ (I Corinthians 3:14).

Third, the personal salvation of the sinner is always referred to in the past tense, "SAVED" (Romans 10:13), while the giving of rewards is in the future at His coming (Revelation 22:12).

In order for a person to have a clear understanding of the difference between eternal life and rewards, please consider the following.

ETERNAL LIFE

The mistake that many people make, especially preachers and scholars, is that they look to themselves or to past, renowned preachers or scholars for their definition of terms instead of to **their life's manual, which is the Bible**.

In order for the Bible to be perfect and eternal, it must have only one author, God, The Holy Spirit.

The Holy Spirit is the only author of the sixty-six inspired library of books, we call the Holy Bible. He used about forty different authors to pen the Bible, which he hovered over and directed. Sometimes He literally dictated the very words they penned.

THE LAW OF THE FIRST MENTION

When the Holy Spirit introduced a new term or practice in His Holy Word, he stopped and defined the term or practice. He was always consistent with that definition while using that term or practice in other books of the Bible.

The holy, eternal God made Adam out of the elements of the earth. Adam was created and **God breathed life into him.**

A lost sinner is dead in trespasses and sin. Just as God quickened Adam, the Bible teaches that our eternal God quickens the dead sinner and **gives** him the gift of eternal life when the sinner responds to the Holy Spirit and receives Jesus as his Saviour. He is born again in the spirit and has the same type of life that our eternal God, his Father, has.

REWARDS

The gift of God is eternal life. The Holy Spirit could not make that truth any clearer. He that receives Jesus Christ **hath eternal life**. The sinner is born of holy seed (divine nature) in the inward, spiritual part of man. That part of man is the holy seed of God and cannot sin. (I John 3:9)

Rewards have nothing to do with eternal life. The sinner received eternal

life when he was born of God in receiving Jesus into his life and heart.

GOD OFFERS TO PAY HIS CHILDREN FOR WORKING FOR HIM

In addition to the gift of God, which makes a person a child of God with eternal life, God pays a saved person to work for Him. Many may say "I've never heard of such a thing." What many in the religious world have heard is if a child of God doesn't live right and work for God then he is in danger of going to hell.

That doctrinal position makes salvation contingent on what the one saved does and not on what God promises to do for those who receive his Son as their Saviour. Any honest person would call what one does in order to stay saved, GOOD WORKS.

> He made that plain – **you are saved by grace**. Then, as the Holy Spirit often does, He attempts to make this absolutely clear, that salvation of a lost sinner from hell is **by grace and grace alone**. He adds, "**Not of works**".

They say this in spite of the plain statement that the sinner is saved by God's grace. The

Biblical definition of grace states that grace stops being grace when works are attempted to be added to God's grace. Paul emphasizes this truth in Romans 11:6 which states, "And if by grace, then is it no more of works: otherwise grace is no more grace. But if it be of works, then is it no more grace: otherwise work is no more work."

This verse states that salvation of the sinner is not a combination of grace and works.

The plain statement of the Holy Spirit, not what a preacher or a renowned theologian says, is "By grace are ye saved through faith and that not of yourselves, it is the gift of God: **not of works**…" Ephesians 2:8-9

He made that plain – **you are saved by grace**. Then, as the Holy Spirit often does, He attempts to make absolutely clear that salvation of a lost sinner from hell is **by grace and grace alone.** He adds, "**Not of works.**" One is not saved by works of any kind.

The Holy Spirit gives the reason that one is not saved by any of his "good works" by adding, "…**lest any man should boast.**"

Jesus died as the sinner's substitute and endured the condemnation of God's wrath on sin by suffering man's pain of hell. God offers salvation as a free gift to any person, by his grace and goodness, providing the sinner acknowledges and turns from his sin to accept Christ as his personal Saviour by faith. The sinner pleads to God, "...**accept the death of Jesus as full payment for my sins and save me a bankrupt, worthless sinner**."

The Holy Spirit is saying, "After Jesus did that for you – after he suffered your judgment and paid for your sins; you are not going to take away any of his glory by strutting around heaven boasting about your good works." **The person would be saying "I made it to heaven when a lot of other weaker, less devoted Christians didn't make it."**

No, Sir, all of us sinners when we get to heaven will sing the same sweet story, **"Saved by His sweet grace."**

SAVED UNTO GOOD WORKS

So, if we are not saved by works, then where does works come in? One is saved by grace "...**unto good works** which God has foreordained that we should walk in them." (Ephesians 2:10)

When a person is truly saved, God has good works for him to do to show that there has been a change in his life.

When one is saved, God has a good, acceptable, and perfect plan all outlined for him to follow. If he humbles himself and follows God's will and pattern for his life then he will receive a "full reward." "http://www.blueletterbible.org/Bible.cfm?b=2Jo&c=1&v=8&t=KJV - comm/8**Look to yourselves, that we lose not those things which we have wrought, but that we receive a full reward.**" II John 1:8

> When a person is truly saved, God has good works for him to do to show that there has been a change in his life.

The rewards will be displayed in the future position one has in THE COMING MILLENNIAL REIGN.

SOME WHO FAILED THE TEST

Esau, as the first born son of Jacob, was offered a full reward and miserably failed the test by selling his birthright to his younger brother. It

> **Solomon** who may have been one of the **greatest young preachers** ever to lead God's people, although warned on several occasions; blew his life, destroyed his family and **lost his future place of greatness.**

is doubtful if Esau was ever saved.

Rueben, the first born son of Israel, also disqualified himself and lost his full reward and probably all rewards.

Solomon, who may have been one of the **greatest young preachers** ever to lead God's people, although warned on several occasions; blew his life, destroyed his family, and **lost his future place of greatness.**

There are more who could be given as examples of those who were offered a "full reward," but were not as wise as Moses who choose to suffer afflictions with God's people rather than enjoy the pleasures of sin for a season. **The name of Moses** shines as brightly as any name in the Old Testament. Esau, Ruben, and Solomon could have shined equally bright, but they got involved in their environment and forfeited their eternal glory. God had a good, acceptable life plan for each of them, but **they refused it and will suffer because of their self centered lives.**

What one does in **this dispensation,** will dictate WHERE he will live in the coming MILLENNIAL DISPENSATION.

God offers each child a full reward to be enjoyed (especially in the Millennium), if he lives as a faithful steward over what God places in his hands. This is taught vividly in the story of **the three servants** *in Matthew 25:14-30.*

He gave each servant according to that servant's ability. All three servants called him **Lord**.

The servant who received five talents **worked faithfully** and gained another five talents.

His Lord, Jesus, rewarded him by saying, "Well done thou good and faithful servant. **Thou hast been faithful over a few things, I will make thee ruler over many things;** enter into the joy of the Lord."

The servant who received two talents **worked faithfully** and gained another two talents.

His Lord, Jesus, rewarded him for his faithful service by saying, **"Well done thou good and faithful servant**, thou hast been faithful over a few things, I will make thee ruler over many things; enter into the joy of the Lord."

The third servant, who received only one talent, called the man "**Lord**" in verse twenty-four. He continues speaking in verse twenty-five that he had no faith (was afraid) and had disobeyed **his Lord's** orders. He hid

his Lord's money in the earth, which is a picture of the world, and returned the one talent to **His Lord.**

THE ABSOLUTE WRATH OF HIS LORD WAS UNLEASHED UPON HIM

Verse twenty-six confirms that this man **was a servant (child of God)**. HIS LORD answered and said unto him, "Thou wicked and slothful [lazy] servant." After his Lord had severely rebuked him, he stripped him of his possession and gave it to the other servant who had worked faithfully.

The Lord then reaffirmed the principle that has been stated previously in other verses. That principle is, God will take from those who do not work and give it to his faithful workers (verse twenty-nine).

The Lord then banishes the unfaithful and lazy servant from his fellowship for 1000 years.

Light represents fellowship, while darkness represents separation. In I John 1:7, it gives the definition of light as fellowship when it states, "…if we walk in **the light,** as he is in

> This ungodly servant was not sent to hell, but the people he hindered from being saved **are in hell**.

the light, we have **fellowship** one with another...."

Ephesians 5:11, admonishes the believer to have no **fellowship** with the unfruitful works of darkness.

This ungodly servant was not sent to hell, but the people he hindered from being saved **are in hell**. The Lord used the word hell in verse forty-one and forty-six, and if he had sent this servant to hell he would have used the word, hell, in verse thirty.

This wicked servant will suffer for 1000 years with the stinging words of his Lord ringing in his ears as he works with the sinners and hypocrites in some place of labor. He will be aware of those that stumbled over his rebellious and self-center life as they suffer in the eternal fires of hell. His sentence is only 1000 years,

> This wicked servant will suffer for 1000 years with the stinging words of his Lord ringing in his ears as he works with the sinner and hypocrites in some place of labor.

which will include witnessing the casting of the lost into the Lake of Fire. It is only after God makes a new Heaven and a new earth that God will graciously **wipe the tears from his unfaithful and wicked children's eyes**. It is recorded in Revelation 21:4,

"…God shall wipe away the tears from their eyes…neither shall there be any more pain; FOR THE FORMER THINGS ARE PASSED AWAY."

With these principles in mind, please consider the tremendous positions of honor that God offers his children who triumph by his grace.

Keep this question in mind as you review the rewards God offers to his children.

"Where will I live across the river?"

Chapter Seven
THOSE WHO WILL TRIUMPH IN THE KINGDOM

To triumph, have God put His stamp of approval upon your life, and hear Him say, "Well done," is the greatest achievement available to man. That is exactly what God offers you and every human being who has ever lived.

That is God's wish and will for you. He designed a good, perfect, and acceptable plan that would end with each person standing in triumph before Him. He longs to bless, to honor, to reward, and say, "Well done, thy good and faithful servant, enter into the joy of thy Lord," to each one of His children. God so desires this for you that He gave His Son to suffer and die in order to make it possible.

> That is God's wish and will for you. For each person, He designed a good, perfect, and acceptable plan that would end with you standing in triumph before Him.

However, so many of His children are distracted by the things of the world and lose their focus as a Christian. Others have never understood the purpose for God offering rewards, while others have been falsely led to believe that just getting to Heaven is a sufficient reward.

The Bible teaches that a person is saved by grace and grace alone. He reinforces that a child of God is saved by grace alone by adding the statement, "Not of works, lest any man should boast." Eph 2:9 However, the Bible is just as plain to point out that every child of God **will be rewarded according to his own works**, as it is to say a sinner is saved by grace.

> Man has an innate desire to win, to succeed, to rise above his fellow man. Why? This is because God designed or programmed him to have dominion or to triumph over the earth.

Because God is a triumphant God, He wants his children to triumph also. God created man to have dominion or triumph over the earth. Gen 1:26

Adam was to have dominion over all the earth and the animal kingdom, and govern them for God. "Thou madest him to have dominion over the works of thy hands; thou host put all things under his feet:" Psalms 8:6

Adam failed and forfeited his lordship when he sinned, but his failure did not change God's purpose for creating man; nor did it change God's plan for man to have dominion and govern the earth for God.

Man has an innate desire to win, to succeed, and to rise above his fellow man. Why? This is because God designed or programmed him to have dominion or to triumph over all the earth.

The devil and the world have captured man's innate nature to excel and have dominion. The devil has done this by getting man to use this driving desire for **self-gratification and gain.**

> The devil and the world have captured man's innate nature to excel and have dominion. The devil has done this by getting man to use this driving desire for **self-gratification and gain.**

This nature to have dominion has been behind every war and every argument. But just because man has used every device, regardless of its brutality, to have dominion over others, it **has not changed God's plan** for man to have dominion over the earth.

MY WAYS ARE NOT MAN'S WAYS

Isaiah, the prophet, stated this principle in *Isaiah 55:8,* man believes "might is right." Get all you can, **regardless of who you hurt.**

In Luke 14, Jesus speaks of a king who plans on going to war, but first determines if he can win with his army. This illustrates the way man considers having dominion. Are we strong enough to win? Can we beat them?

Jesus told the apostles that, "This philosophy is the way of the world, **but it shall not be so with you."** Then He stated something that is contrary to man's reasoning. He said that the one, who would become great, **let him be a minister** (server); and that he who would become chief (have dominion), **let him become a servant.** Matt 20:25-28

Paul commented on this reasoning in Philippians, Chapter 2, where he stated that Jesus was on the same level with God, but humbled Himself and took upon Himself the form of a servant.

> He said that the one who would become great, **let him be a minister** (server); and that he who would become chief (have dominion), **let him become a servant.**

Then Paul gives the results of Jesus' humility by saying, "Wherefore God also hath **highly exalted him,** and given him a name which is above every name." Philippians 2:9 The key line of this illustration is, "Let this mind be in you, which was also in Christ Jesus." Phil 2:5

Peter admonished pastors to be clothed with humility. He commanded ministers to, "Humble yourselves therefore under the mighty hand of God, that he may exalt you in due time [either later in life or in the Millennium]." I Peter 5:6

He states that, "the God of all grace, **who hath called us unto his eternal glory by Christ Jesus,** after that ye have suffered a while, make you perfect, stablish, strengthen, settle you." I Peter 5:10

Jesus preached that if a man was going to follow Him and be one of His disciples, then he had to deny himself and take up the cross (purpose of life). If a man would do this, Jesus said, He would save his life (of service). But if a man saved his life for himself and the things he wanted to do, **then he would lose (or misspend) his life.**

Jesus then made the statement that so many misinterpret, "What profit a man if he gains the whole world, but loses or misspends his life of service?"

Jesus asked this very pointed question that is generally misinterpreted, "What would a man give to go back after he had gained the whole world, at the expense of missing God's will and misspending his life (his purpose on this earth) to live a humble, submissive life for Christ?"

> He has lived his whole life for himself, at the expense of his service for Christ and he will stand before Christ ashamed!

Now, he must face what Jesus states in Mark 8:38, that he has lived his whole life for himself, at the expense of his service for Christ and he will stand before Christ ashamed! Jesus said, "Whosoever therefore [because of his misspent life] shall be ashamed of me and my words in this adulterous and sinful generation; of him also shall the Son of man be ashamed, when he cometh in the glory of his Father with the holy angels." Mark 8:38

Man's way is to win by strength; God's way is to win **by giving his life in service**. Man's way is to win by taking; God's way is **to win by giving**. Man's way is to get what he cannot keep; God's way is **to give what His servant cannot lose**.

God's great desire for His children is to help them, by His grace, to have dominion and rule over this earth with Him. The way to achieve this and a have a full reward (II John 8) and the Lord's "well done" at the Judgment Seat is expressed in this old song: **"Let me lose my life and find it Lord, in thee. In my life, may my friends see only thee. Though it cost me grief and pain, I will find my life again. Let me lose my life and find it Lord, in thee."**

> God's way is to win by giving his life in service.

For the obedient, there will be many great positions of triumph and fellowship during the Millennial Reign of Christ. In order to illustrate these different positions of triumph and leadership, the author **will refer to these positions as "clubs."** Bear in mind, **there will not** be any such clubs in the Millennium. The author is calling the various levels of rewards "clubs" in order to illustrate the various levels of leadership positions that will be honored in the Millennium.

There are some positions that hold greater authority and honor than other positions, but all reflect great triumph and achievement. Please study these suggested levels in the light in which the author offers them - **to give emphasis to the fact** that God will greatly reward those who deny themselves, take up the cross (work), and follow their Lord.

The entry to all levels of recognition begins at the Judgment Seat of Christ, where each Christians' works **will be tried by fire.**

First, everyone at this judgment has the right foundation, which is Christ. 1 Cor 3:11 This means that all of them have accepted Christ as their Savior. Jesus is the foundation of every Christian's life.

> The entry to all levels of recognition begins at the Judgment Seat of Christ, where every Christians' works will be tried by fire.

The Christian then begins to build his life upon this true foundation. If he builds with the materials of wood, hay or stubble, **his works will be tested by fire and burned up**. His whole life's work will be reduced to ashes, "...but he himself shall be saved; yet so as by fire." I Corinthians 3:15

But if he builds upon his true foundation, works that will honor and glorify Christ, **then he will be rewarded and honored.**

TRIED AND TESTED CLUB

Those who will triumph will have built their life's work upon Jesus, according to His direction and Word. Their building materials will be gold, silver and precious stones. The judgment fires of testing will be applied to their works also, but will only burn out the dross and purify the materials. These tried and tested members will at least have some reward and commendation from their Savior. There will be a "well done."

Please note that this promise is in the abstract because it is referring to every believer who will appear before the Judgment Seat of Christ. But when you study this promise of reward in the light of other promises, you will find that rewards promised to individuals are concrete, while general promises of reward are in the abstract. "...every man shall receive his own reward according to his own labour."
I Corinthians 3:8

Many of these will go on to the highest level of triumph and glory, but all will enter into the Millennium to rule with Jesus. Some will have saved more of their life than others, but all of them will have their works tried and tested and will enter into the realm of those who are triumphing in Jesus.

100 FOLD CLUB

Some will Qualify to Occupy a Position in the 100 Fold Club

The 100 Fold Club is promised to every believer who has forsaken their lands, families, jobs and personal ambitions in order to follow Jesus in carrying out the Gospel and winning souls. They have done it for Jesus sake. In Matt 19:29, Jesus promised them a pay check of 100 fold, which would be an everlasting inheritance.

> "Every man shall receive his own reward according to his own labor."

The subject under consideration is rewards or pay checks for serving Christ. Peter and the apostles told Jesus that they had forsaken all and then asked Him, "...what shall we have therefore [or because of this sacrifice]?"Matt 19:27

Jesus promised that their reward would be to sit upon twelve thrones and judge Israel for 1000 years.

The subject is a pay check (rewards), not salvation. One does not inherit everlasting life. Everlasting life is a free gift, which is offered by the grace of God and accepted by faith. To Christians who have accepted Jesus as their Savior by faith, God

> The subject is a pay check (rewards), not salvation. One does not inherit everlasting life. Everlasting life is a free gift.

gives eternal life. But for those Christians who have forsaken families, jobs, lands, and personal ambitions in order to get people saved, God promises to give them an inheritance of upward to 100 fold.

Please note that this promise is in the abstract, as far as talking to people, "everyone," but it is in the concrete as to the percentage of return on their investments, 100 fold.

Whatever personal gain a person forsakes, he will be paid 100 fold. Whatever he gives through tithes and offerings, God promises to repay him 100 fold. A reader may reason, "100% of what one gives? Boy, what a great rate of interest!" But 100

> 10,000 times what they have forsaken for Jesus in order to obey Him and 10,000 times what they gave through tithes and offerings.

fold does not mean that your investment's return is 100%. It is ten thousand (10,000) times what the person gave or invested! What a tremendous return for the ones who obeyed the command of laying up treasures in Heaven! Ten thousand times what they have forsaken for Jesus in obeying Him and ten thousand times what they gave through tithes and offerings. In earthly language, some of these people would be millionaires. In Heavenly language, they are fulfilling God's plan for their lives – to have dominion over the earth.

It doesn't matter whether you describe their rewards in earth's language or in Heaven's. The bottom line is that they are numbered with the saints that have triumphed, **and it will be an everlasting inheritance.**

HELPER'S CLUB

Many have a mistaken belief that a person has to do something great before he would be in line for a reward. No doubt, the devil shoots this misinformation into the average person's mind for them to draw back in disbelief.

> He does this by pointing out and exaggerating the merits of the other person's life and accusing him of his failures and shortcomings.

The devil wages war against the Christian's mind by trying to magnifying what someone else does and at the same time exploiting the Christian's poor self image by minimizing his works. He does this by pointing out and exaggerating the merits of the other person's life and accusing him of his failures and shortcomings.

It is true that some people have greater abilities and talents than others. Paul, speaking of a local church, referred to it as a human body. He said that the body is not one member, but many. I Cor 12:14

Then Paul explained that, "God set the members every one of them in the body, as it hath pleased him." I Cor 2:18 He was teaching that the church is a team and every member of the church is part of the team. From the most talented to the least, all work together and are important. He stated that the smallest part of the body is absolutely necessary for the proper working of the team. He stated something that **every member, who has been lied to by the devil regarding their usefulness to the team, should treasure.** He said, "And those members of the body [church], which we think to be less honourable [important], **upon these we bestow more abundant honuor; and our uncomely parts** [less attractive as far as ability] have more abundant comeliness... but God hath tempered the body together, having given more abundant honour to that part which lacked." 1 Cor 12:23-24

Now that is how God looks at each member of the church, or team. The **most insignificant member is important to God and, He especially wants to bless him.**

A person who has less talent can become part of the Helpers Club in many ways.

One who helps a prophet (preacher) shall receive a prophet's reward. Matt 10:41 We may help in babysitting for the preacher's kids. We may help by giving them a ride to church. We may help by cleaning the house or mowing the yard.

One who helps a righteous man (a fellow Christian) shall receive a righteous man's reward. If a fellow Christian's house is flooded, pitch in and help clean up the mess. If there is sickness in a fellow member's family, go sit with them in the hospital or take them food. There are many things a person can do that will place him in the Helpers Club. Jesus promised a reward to anyone who would give a cold glass of water to one of His little ones. Matt 10:42

> One who helps a prophet (preacher) shall receive a prophet's reward.

Paul told the Philippian church that they were in the Helpers Club when they supported him as a missionary. Read what the great preacher said, "Not because I desire a gift: but I desire fruit that may abound to your account." Phil 4:17

He was telling those dear people who supported his ministry that by doing so, it enabled him to win more people to the Lord. Paul rejoiced that those people, who helped him, would also share in the rewards for getting people saved. He also rejoiced because he knew that by their sacrificial gifts, they would be elevated some day and live in triumph as members of the Helpers Club.

Remember, your gifts do not have to be a huge amount to get God's attention. Remember the story of the widow in Luke, Chapter 21, who gave her two mites. Jesus said that **she had given more** than anyone else that day.

So come on you members, who consider yourselves to be just average, and who don't think you have any talent. Help the preacher, support the missionaries, or help a dear brother in need. There is plenty of room in the Helpers Club, and the club is now accepting members.

This promise, in the abstract, is attempting to get what many think is the common man, or little guy's attention. It is also an abstract reward in what the prophet or righteous man receives if he gives his all, even if his all is two mites. **But it is a concrete promise from Almighty God** that He is aware of your help and will give you a reward for doing it.

RULER OF MANY THINGS CLUB

In the example Jesus used in Matthew 25, He gave servants talents according to their different abilities. When He came back to have them give an account of their stewardship, He said the same thing to the two servants who had been faithful and used their talents, regardless of how many they had been given. He said "...Well done, thou good and faithful servant: thou hast been faithful over a few things, I will make thee ruler over many things; enter thou into the joy of thy lord." Matt 25:21 and 23

Again, this means that some may have more of the "many things" or talents, but all that enter into this category, by using their abilities for the Lord, will triumph and enter into the joy of "thy Lord."

This should be very encouraging to many of God's children who don't think they have any talent. It stresses being faithful over whatever talent one has. One does not have to compete with someone who is more talented for a reward. If he works faithfully with his limited talents in the place God has put him, God will place him in a position of service in the Millennium, where he will enjoy his life in triumph.

This promise of reward is in the abstract because it states "ruler of many things." But when one considers the concrete promise of being ruler over five or ten cities, it makes it a concrete promise. It causes one to adjust his thinking upward to "ruler over many things."

FIVE POUND CLUB

In Luke 19, Jesus tells about giving ten servants one pound (money) each and telling them to do business "until I come." When He returned, one of the servants had advanced his **one pound to five pounds.** The scripture states, "And the second came, saying, Lord, thy pound hath gained five pounds. And He [Jesus] said likewise to him, Be thou also over five cities." Luke

19:18-19

This teaches that those who work for the Lord have the possibility of triumphing by being **made ruler over five cities**.

When one studies this story, it seems like the second servant could have done better. He was given one pound, just as the other servants were given one pound. The first servant received a ringing commendation from the Lord, who said "...Well, thou good servant...." whereas the Lord did not commend the second servant as highly. He only said, "...Be thou also over five cities." which seems to indicate that there **were some lapses in this person's life of service.** He may not have heeded the warning found in 11 John 1:8, which says, "Look to yourselves, that we lose not those things which we have wrought [gained], but that we receive a full reward."

> *"And He [Jesus] said likewise to him, Be thou also over five cities." Luke 19:18-19*

This may have been put in the Bible for those Christians who have not **maintained their committed, faithful service to Christ.** They may have dropped off in their giving. Maybe they stopped soul-winning, or their lives are not as faithful as they had once been.

If this is true for you, then you may not be commended like the man who had earned ten pounds. But you can go back to work for Christ and still triumph. Maybe the reward will not be over ten cities, or even five cities, but you can still recover and be rewarded instead of losing your reward.

> But you can go back to work for Christ and still triumph. Maybe the reward will not be over ten cities, or even five cities, but you can still recover and be rewarded instead of losing your reward.

Look to yourself and serve the Lord. His will for you is to reign with Him as a triumphant servant. The Five Pound Club will still be a place of victory and joy for 1000 years.

This is an absolute promise made to an individual who may not have received a full reward, but being over five cities for 1000 years is a tremendous reward.

A BETTER RESURRECTION CLUB

In Hebrews 11:3-5, right in the middle of the list of the great heroes of faith in the Old Testament, is a motivational

statement. It is found in the midst of such descriptions of persecutions as:
- They had trials of cruel mocking and scourging
- They were in bonds and imprisonment
- Some were stoned
- Some were sawn asunder
- Many were slain with the sword
- Others were destitute, afflicted, tormented

The motivational statement for such endurance of pain is "...not accepting deliverance; that they might obtain a better resurrection." Heb 11:35 This **"better resurrection" refers to a better position in the 1000-year reign.**

The apostle Paul spoke about his driving desire to advance in the order of the resurrection. He

> The motivational statement for such endurance of pain is "...not accepting deliverance; that they might obtain a better resurrection." Heb 11:35

spoke of having fellowship with His (Jesus') suffering and being conformable to His death. This means he wished to die like Jesus died, or at least die for Him. Phil 3:10

Why suffer and die for Jesus? He answered, "In order to obtain a better resurrection." Then Paul was quick to add, "Not that I haven't already attained, but that I may have a higher position in the resurrection." Phil 3:11-12

> As an old man, he was still working hard for the Lord. He was totally committed to suffering and even death if he could obtain a better resurrection.

As an old man, he was still working hard for the Lord. He was totally committed to suffering and even death if he could obtain a better resurrection. In fact, Paul didn't just want a better resurrection, he wanted to be first or have the highest position in the resurrection. Listen to his famous desire, "I press toward the mark for the prize of the high [upward] calling of God in Christ Jesus." Phil 3:14

The Lord placed this desire in Paul's heart, because Paul was one of the worst sinners ever saved to work and to demonstrate how to become first or at least among the first, in the resurrection. God not

> Personal discomfort and suffering did not distract him in his pursuit of a better resurrection.

only used Paul as an example of triumph, but to show all other sinners the steps that one must take to advance in the Better Resurrection Club - **abandonment of self and a total dedication to the Lord.** Personal discomfort and suffering did not distract Paul in his pursuit of a better resurrection.

From this Better Resurrection Club group, who loved Christ more than their own lives, will come the one who will obtain the greatest reward and honor at the Judgment Seat. Paul strove to be the best, or first in the Better Resurrection Club. In doing this, he inspired thousands by his total dedication to his Lord.

This total dedication will place Paul **in a place of close, daily fellowship with his Lord for the full coming 1000 years**. Other saints also chose to suffer for Christ because of their love for Him and their desire to have this personal, daily fellowship

AUTHOR'S NOTE: The author does not mean that some were working to be a "big shot" in the 1000-year reign with Jesus. No, I believe they were working in order to receive the supreme reward one will have in the 1000-year reign, **a nearness to Jesus where they can serve him more intimately.**

TEN CITIES CLUB

In Luke Chapter 19, the first servant who received one pound had increased his Lord's money to ten pounds. When this report was made, his Lord said unto him "...Well, thou good servant: because thou hast been faithful in a very little, have thou authority over ten cities." Luke 19:17

Having authority over ten cities and ruling them for the Lord Jesus Christ, would certainly place one in great triumph as an area governor. Boss or ruler with Jesus for the entire 1000-year reign will be a great reward for the Lord's faithful servants.

Please note the following observation. This person started at the same level with all of the Lord's servants. **They each had one pound.** This does not indicate that he had greater or lesser abilities than the other nine servants. His accomplishment seems to **indicate his faithfulness and focus** in working for his master. His reward is a **direct result of his faithfulness and hard work.**

His faithfulness placed him in a leadership position in the Millennium, ruler or boss over ten cities. He may not have had the greatest talent, but he worked and was always faithful. He may be **the best role model** for you to follow in striving to join the Five Pound Club. **So go for it!** Strive

> His accomplishment seems to indicate **his faithfulness and focus** in working for his master. His reward seems to be a **direct result of his faithfulness and hard work.**

to become part of the Ten Cities Club. Remember, **rewards are offered to motivate people to work**. It pleases God to honor and reward those that do. This is a concrete promise to those who will strive to be true and faithfully serve Christ.

THE "ALL STARS" CLUB

God used one of his great prophets, Daniel, to look beyond the Judgment Seat of Christ and single out the **stars in the "All Stars" Club.** Hundreds of years before the birth of Christ, Daniel spoke of the **stars that would shine forever and ever.** These "All Stars" are those who had won souls to Christ and then trained them in discipleship.

King David was a man after God's own heart because **he was a soul winner.** When he repented of the horrible sin that almost wrecked his life he said, "God, if you will forgive me and restore the joy of thy salvation, "Then will I teach transgressors thy ways; and sinners shall be converted unto thee [I'll go back to the thing dearest to your heart - getting sinners saved]." Ps 51:13

> He may not have had the greatest talent, but he worked and was always faithful. He may be **the best role model** for you to follow.

Solomon, his son, who is reputed to be the wisest man to ever live, said, "…he that winneth souls is wise." Pro 11:30

Daniel saw those wise men as shining stars. He saw those who trained and taught people how to live and serve Jesus, as stars that would shine forever and ever. His exact vision was, "And they that be

> Those who think that soul winning will not work in today's society better rethink that conclusion.

wise [soul winners] shall shine as the brightness of the firmament; and they that turn many to righteousness [winning and teaching] **as the stars for ever and ever."** Dan 12: 3

Many think that soul winning is a modern day term and practice. Soul winning is an Old Testament term. God, the Father, was the first soul winner when He came seeking Adam and Eve.

Those who think that soul winning will not work in today's society better rethink that conclusion. Those who will triumph the most at the Judgment Seat, are those who will follow the example of Jesus. **He came to seek and to save those which were lost**. Then He commanded his church, "...as my Father hath sent me, even so send I you." John 20:21

A star or "All Star" on any level is someone who is excelling. But a star or "All Star" on the Lord's team during the 1000-year reign and on into the eternal age is someone, who by the grace of God has really triumphed.

It is fitting that God rewards the ones who discovered what life is all about, reaching men with the gospel. **These are the ones He elevates to His "All Stars" Club**.

This is a concrete promise, although it is written to all that are "wise" (soul-winners). It is clear that God will pick His "All Stars" from those **who have made a priority of reaching men with the Gospel**.

THE EXCLUSIVE CLUB

As in all societies, there are clubs for handpicked people. You will find at least one such club in the 1000-year reign of

Christ on this earth. Jesus is the one who hand picked the members Himself.

When the threat of death was so great to anyone who attended one of Jesus' meetings, the crowds became small. The apostles became discouraged and began to discuss among themselves what they would gain by following Jesus for the past three and one half years. Jesus provoked them into asking what they were going to be paid for giving up everything to follow Him. Matt 19:27 Jesus promptly answered them by making the following promise, "And I appoint unto **you a kingdom,** as my Father hath appointed unto me; That ye may eat and drink at my table **in my kingdom,** and sit on thrones judging the twelve tribes of Israel." Luke 22:29-30

> It is clear that God will pick His "All Stars" from those who have made a priority of reaching men with the Gospel.

> As in all societies, there are clubs for handpicked people. You will find at least one such club in the 1000-year reign

Thus we have the origin of the Exclusive Club. The apostle Peter will become KING PETER and rule over one of the twelve tribes of Israel for the entire

1000-year reign. The apostle John will become KING JOHN; the apostle James will become KING JAMES; and so on.

This serves as a perfect example of Jesus' desire to make people priests and kings. Rev 1:6 These

> Most of the apostles gave their physical lives in order to secure their place in this **Exclusive Club.**

positions of priests and kings will fulfill God's great desire for man to have dominion over the earth.

No wonder these twelve apostles turned the world upside down in order to preach the Gospel to their generation. Most of the apostles gave their physical lives in order to secure their place in this **Exclusive Club.** They could not take their **minds off of what they had to look forward to for 1000 years - to** eat and drink at their Master's table and **be in the presence of the One they loved so dearly.**

The promise made to the apostles, that if they completed their work, then they would eat and drinks at His table and sit on a throne for 1000 years was so concrete in their mind, that no one was able to ever distract them from their purpose.

DECISION MAKING CLUB

One famous President was noted for his straight forwardness in making decisions. His famous saying was, "The buck stops here." This statement means he couldn't shirk his responsibility for making decisions any longer.

During the Millennial Reign of Christ, Jesus will place some men in **the decision making position of absolute authority**. The buck will stop at their throne, as they run part of the world for the King of Kings. Listen to Jesus' statement to these special people who triumphed. "And he that overcometh, and keepeth my works unto the end, to him **will I give power over the nations:** And he shall **rule them with a rod of iron;** as the vessels of a potter shall they be broken to shivers: even as I received of my Father." Rev 2:26-27

Can you imagine a lowly preacher, missionary, or Christian worker being raised and promoted to such a prominent decision making position? **To literally rule part of the world with absolute authority**, with no one to answer to, but Jesus or one of His executive committee members? By one's humility, obedience, and God's grace, he has reached one of the highest levels of triumph **ever offered to man.**

Note the expression: "he that overcometh." This plainly teaches that there were problems, pressures, and great difficulties to overcome. To be in this club, one must become an overcomer. One overcomes by faith as he submits to God's grace and trusts in the promises found in God's Word.

Note the expression: "keeps my work unto the end." One must keep working; regardless of the pain and suffering he endures. Frances Ashbury, a circuit-riding preacher at the age of 91, would ride a horse up into the mountains in order to preach to the distant villages. **He would exclaim, "Pain, pain, pain!" as he rode his horse into the mountains where hundreds were saved.**

Jesus promises that if one would overcome and do His work until the end, he would triumph and help rule the earth for 1000 years.

In the torturous conditions which millions of God's children live, nothing but the concrete promises of God can sustain them.

EXECUTIVE CLUB

There may be many other levels of triumphs and glory that we have not mentioned, but the last level of triumph that we will consider here is the Executive Club.

This club will be made up of those whom Jesus likes to refer to as overcomers. He defines overcomers as those who by faith have overcome every level of test and problem that they ever encountered - **and were victorious.** He will say to that group that He will allow them to sit with Him on His throne as He is sat down with His father on His throne. His very words are "To him that overcometh **will I grant to sit with me in my throne,** even as I also overcame, and am set down with my Father in his throne." Rev 3:21 **This statement places some in the Executive Club.**

> "To him that overcometh **will I grant to sit with me in my throne,** even as I also overcame, and am set down with my Father in his throne."

An old Southern country farmer would say, "Now **that** is high cotton!" While the city slicker would exclaim, "Sitting on the Executive Board to rule the world with Jesus as Chairman of the

Board, now **that is the greatest, the greatest!"**

Any way one looks at it or expresses it, obtaining that lofty position is one of the highest triumphs imaginable to man. This is the position that God has created to show His gratitude and appreciation to those who have made the greatest sacrifices in obeying His command, "go into the whole world and preach the Gospel to every creature."

In our modern day world, where millions of our brothers and sisters in third world countries are suffering and dying for our Lord, there is nothing to sustain them other than God's grace and the concrete promises of God. These poor people are largely ignored by this generation, but they will shine brightly in the soon coming 1000-year reign.

> These poor people in third-world countries are largely ignored by this generation, but they will shine brightly in the soon coming 1000 year reign.

GOD WORKS TOWARD A GOAL OR PURPOSE

The Bible clearly teaches that God set goals and has a purpose for all of His children to fulfill. He promises certain rewards for those who accomplish their purpose, which we have illustrated in this chapter. We have tried to spark your imagination to study the purpose for which you are saved.

A GREAT REWARD FOR THOSE WHO HAVE FAILED AS A CHRISTIAN

This is contrary to the laws which **govern the giving of rewards, BUT IT IS TRUE!**

This section's heading, "**A great reward for those who have failed as a Christian,**" is made just to get the reader's attention, create curiosity, and give people **who have all but made shipwreck of their lives new hope.** This promise was made by Jesus himself and merits our greatest consideration.

> This exception to the rule, which governs the earning of rewards, was made to a particular group of people at a certain time **for a definite purpose**.

This exception to the rule, which governs the earning of rewards, was made to a particular group of people **for a definite purpose**.

- This Promise was made **by Jesus**
- The Promise was made **to the Eleventh Hour Christians**
- This promise was made **to give people a second chance** as they respond to Jesus' plea to enter into the last harvest and win souls
- This promise was made in order **to help save the six and one-half billion** harvest of lost souls.
- This promise is found in **Matthew 20:1-16,** and will be fully explained in a later chapter of this book.

This promise is an exception to the rule of giving rewards because it is made to a certain group of people. It was made to those who had been **all the day standing idle.** That is, up until this point they had not been

> It may have been something in their past that disqualified them from working in the Lord's vineyard, perhaps a broken marriage, or they made shipwreck of their lives.

working for the Lord, but were lukewarm or bench warming church members.

When Jesus asked them why they had been standing all the day idle, they answered

"BECAUSE NO MAN HATH HIRED US." It may have been because they were looked down upon for something in their life. It may have been that they felt unworthy. It may have been something in their past that disqualified them from working in the Lord's vineyard, perhaps a broken marriage, or they made shipwreck of their lives.

Regardless of why, Jesus told them to go to work in his vineyard even though it was the Eleventh Hour with just one hour before the day or the dispensation ended.

> This exception to the rule was made in order to hire workers in the last few days of this age that will help save part of the six and one-half billion lost souls.

These workers, hired at the Eleventh Hour, were the first workers paid. They were **shocked when they received a FULL DAY'S PAY**.

When all of the workers who had labored in the harvest were paid, they each received the **same wages, a full days pay**. This does not mean that everyone at the Judgment seat will be rewarded the same. We have already seen that every man will be rewarded **according to his own labor.**

This illustration was made in order to motivate workers in the last few days of this age. To motivate a life change in them from being idle to being workers that will help save part of the six and one-half billion lost souls.

The message from Jesus is the harvest is perishing, time is running out, and regardless of your past wasted life, I will pay you as if you had worked all day IF YOU WILL THROW YOURSELF INTO THE HARVEST BY WINNING SOULS.

Jesus came to save sinners from hell. There are six and one-half to seven billion people on the earth and a vast number of them still lost. With time running out **Jesus "ups the ante" as far as rewards are concerned**. He uses the same strategy, which stimulated the apostles in an all out effort. **After all, he died to save sinners.** That is the most important thing to Jesus, the thing closest to his heart - **To seek and to save that which is lost!**

He doesn't want to rebuke and punish his children at the Judgment Seat for their wasted and unfruitful lives. What good would that do? Many sinners will have already died and have gone to hell by that point.

He offers the people in the Eleventh Hour **a chance to recover their lives** by going into the harvest of six and one-half billion so many lost sinners will escape hell and have eternal life.

The end result will be two fold. Many more sinners will be saved from hell and many of his children's lives will be salvaged. They will be victorious and rewarded instead of punished at the Judgment Seat.

When questioned why he would pay someone a whole day's pay for working but one hour, he said, "Is it not lawful for me to do what I will with my own?" In that statement he is stating, **"I am the sovereign Lord of the harvest, and I can do as I please with my own."** It is very clear that he was willing to do everything in his power to save as much of the harvest as possible. He is willing to use anyone, regardless of their past, to get people saved from hell.

> **The end result will be two fold.** Many more sinners will be saved from hell and many of his children's lives will be salvaged. They will be victorious and rewarded instead of punished at the judgment seat.

In this story he is willing to use a person who has been wasting his life, even to the point of giving him complete amnesty for the past, and then pay him as though he had worked all of his life if…**if…IF HE WILL DO EVERYTHING IN HIS POWER TO SAVE THE LOST SINNERS WHO MAKE UP OUR PRESENT DAY HARVEST!**

Chapter Eight
THOSE WHO WILL SHED TEARS IN THE KINGDOM PART A

In this chapter, we will deal with the pain that many of God's children will endure throughout the Millennial Reign. Every knee will bow and every tongue will confess the Lordship of Jesus at the Judgment Seat of Christ.

> Many of the people of our modern Christian world are in for a shock when they stand before the Lord at the Judgment Seat of Christ.

Many of the people of our modern Christian world are in for a shock when they stand before the Lord at the Judgment Seat of Christ. The author is not trying to be judgmental, but **writing with the hope of alerting people of what lies ahead**. If a person, who has been careless in his Christian life, prayerfully reads this and responds to the Lord's direction, it should help his status in the Millennium and elevate **where he will live on the other side of the river.**

In our first section, we will examine the judgment that will produce pain to the populace as they face the ordeal of "ashes only."

In the second section, we will show the ordeal that the unfaithful Christians, who were **parents,** will face. "Something worse than death" awaits many worldly, unfaithful parents; and it concerns their most precious possession, their children.

THE PAIN OF THE POPULACE, "ASHES ONLY"

As a little boy, my whole life was changed **by fire.** Our family went from a moderately successful farming family to a bankrupt family, in one night, by the **burning of our huge barn.** The yearly crops were all gathered within the barn and the insurance had lapsed the thirty-first of the previous month. Everything was gone in one fire. **Everything was turned to ashes.** This is exactly the pain that many of God's rebellious children will face - **the pain of ashes only.**

> Everything was gone in one fire. **Everything was turned to ashes.** This is exactly the pain that many of God's rebellious children will face - **the pain of ashes**

SAVED SO AS BY FIRE

In I Cor 3:10-15, the apostle Paul admonishes believers to be careful what materials they use in building their Christian life. He lists six different materials: **gold, silver, precious stones, wood, hay and stubble** - "…and the fire shall try every man's work of what sort it is. If any man's work abide which he hath built thereupon, he shall receive a reward. If any man's work shall be burned, he shall suffer loss: but he himself shall be saved; yet so as by fire." verse 13-15

> They did not save any of their time, any of their money, any of their life - it is all gone - ashes only.

He will be saved and go into the Millennial Reign and then on into the eternal age, but **he will suffer loss of rewards**. No doubt, some people will have "ashes only." Everything will be gone, but they will be saved – "so as by fire."

Their whole life's work - GONE! They will stand before their Lord ashamed and naked. They did not save any of their time, any of their money, any of their life – it is all gone, **there are ashes only.**

SNATCHED FROM THE FIRE

In Jude, the Bible speaks of some Christians who were "snatched from the fire," meaning literally saved from hell at the last moment or opportunity. Jude 23

Many people will go to the Judgment Seat as a person who was saved late in life or just before they died. All of their sins were paid for by the blood of Jesus, but there was little or no time for them to work for the Lord.

There will be great joy that they are in Heaven. They will have a fresh start in the Millennial Reign as a newborn child of God, starting out in a new life. Snatched from the fires of hell, to learn and live for Jesus in His personal Kingdom and throughout the age to come. Snatched by grace from the fires of hell to live forever and praise Jesus. How marvelous is our Savior!

> Snatched by grace from the fires of hell to forever live and praise Jesus. How marvelous is our Savior!

PURIFIED BY FIRE

The author's belief is that a lot of Christians who have had a set back and sinned, like King David, will be purified by the fire and go into **the Kingdom victorious and rejoicing.**

When one studies the lives of Old Testament Saints, such as Abraham, one can see the frailty of the flesh. They were just humans in the process of learning to walk and follow God by faith. There were sins and mistakes, but in the New Testament **there is no mention** of those sins or mistakes.

I believe those Christians will be purified by fire and go into the 1000-year Kingdom **with joy and triumph.** They overcame their weakness and frailty and through faith began to grow spiritually. One finds the severity of God's judgment is always connected with a **willful sin or refusing to follow God's will.**

> God's judgment is always connected with a **willful sin** or refusing to follow **God's will.**

The Bible teaches that many of God's children who had a lapse or a breakdown in their Christian life were chastised and learned from that experience. Their overall desire was to serve the Lord. Their motives were right. Jesus will judge at the

> They will suffer the pain and poverty of "ashes only."

Judgment Seat, taking into consideration all aspects of the breakdown, and will reward these Christians based upon what works remain. They will go into the Kingdom **to serve their King joyfully and with honor.** But, the rebellious, willful, worldly children of God, will have their work tried by fire and will go empty handed into their assignment. They will labor with their conscience and the memories of their deeds for 1000 years. They will suffer the pain and poverty of "ashes only."

Isaiah quotes God concerning the religious services, which God totally rejects: "When ye come to appear before me, who hath required this at your hand, to tread my courts? Bring no more vain oblations; incense is an abomination unto me; the new moons and sabbaths, the calling of assemblies, I cannot away with; it is iniquity, even the solemn meeting. Your new moons and your appointed feasts my soul hateth: they are a trouble unto me; I am weary to bear them. And when ye spread forth your hands, I will hide mine eyes from you: yea, when ye make many prayers, I will not hear: your hands are full of blood. Wash you, make you clean; put away the evil of your doings from before mine eyes; cease to do evil;" Isaiah 1:12-16

LOOK TO GOD'S REACTION

They were busy with their "church work," but never did anything to influence sinners to be saved. In Isa. 1:12, we have God's same reaction to many of the church services today. Their order of services is great, the musicians are talented, and to outward appearances it is a great worship service. That is man's view, but God sees the heart, **and is appalled**.

There will be many surprises at the Judgment Seat of Christ. Many church members who seemed to be good Christians will have their motives for serving Christ **tried by fire, and their works will be found as wood, hay, or stubble.** Some people who were barely recognized by the majority of their generation will shine brightly as their works are cleansed and revealed to be Christ-centered and true. Others who served as their leaders or supervisors will weep when the judgment fires burn their works and leave **"ashes only."**

They will weep over their carnal, traditional life which, when tried by the pure judgment fires will reveal a self-serving life. They will realize how hurtful and destructive their religion was as the judgment fires render their works and life to "ashes only."

PARENTS WHO WILL FACE SOMETHING WORSE THAN DEATH

Many parents will face something worse than death, and it will involve their dearest possession, their children.

In our modern day thinking, death is the worse thing that could happen to a person. Someone may ask, "What could happen to a person that would be worse than dying?" We will go through a verse by verse study in order to answer this question.

REVEALING TO PARENTS A PUNISHMENT WHICH IS WORSE THAN DEATH

In Hebrews Chapter10, beginning in verse 22, we have several verses that are clearly speaking to the saved. But many have a tendency, when they come to a verse **that crosses their traditional way of thinking, to apply that verse to the lost.** Many do this in spite of Peter's warning that one can't interpret a scripture by taking it out of context in order to make it fit one's preconceived view. Please carefully study the verses, beginning with verse twenty-two. We will use enough of these verses to prove our point.

Verse 22: "Let us draw near with a true heart," – speaking to the saved.

Verse 23: "Let us hold fast the profession of our faith," – speaking to the saved.

Verse 24: "Let us consider one another," – speaking to the saved.

Verse 25: "Not forsaking the assembling of ourselves together," – again, speaking to the saved.

Verse 26: "For if we sin willfully after that we have received the knowledge of the truth," – Many want to apply this verse to the Jews, but he is still speaking to the saved.

Verse 27: "But a certain fearful looking for of judgment," – still speaking to the saved.

Verse 28: "He that despised Moses' law [one of the Ten Commandments] died without mercy [was stoned to death] under two or three witnesses." – This historical fact happened over and over again in the history of the Jews. This is good illustration that Paul draws from the Old Testament in order to prove his point.

Verse 29: "Of how much sorer punishment," [something worse than death] – still speaking to the saved.

What are the offenses that will bring something to the child of God that is worse than death? Paul listed three of these offenses:

- Trod under foot of the Son of man (Jesus)
- Count the blood of Christ an unholy thing
- Do respite unto the spirit of grace

Some would instantly object and state that a child of God could not do any of those things. Let me restate that in a more accurate statement. You, as a faithful child of God, with your

> "For if **we** sin willfully after that we have received the knowledge of the truth...." - Many want to apply this verse to the Jews, but he is still speaking to the saved.

experience and spiritual condition may not do any of these things. But the child of God, who refuses to surrender to the will of God for his life, and turns back to the world, as Lot did, certainly could and does do these things. In the world, **some children of God become addicted to alcohol, drugs, or sex** and live lives which are shameful and contrary to Biblical standards.

There are children of God who are saved, but become offended in a church split or a broken marriage, and stop going to church. They will soon have their spirituality robbed by their unforgiving attitude and bitterness. That child of God soon begins to resist the leading of the Holy Spirit. His life and conversation soon begins to bring disgrace to himself and to Christ. **The flesh begins to take over and dominates his life**.

> But the child of God, who refuses to surrender to the will of God for his life and turns back to the world, as Lot did, certainly could and does do these things.

Given a few years, this unforgiving attitude and bitterness will rule his life, and he will soon:

- Trod underfoot the Son of God by resisting His leadership
- Do things that will cause the blood of Christ to appear unholy

- Resist and respite the Holy Spirit

At the Judgment Seat, we will learn of all of the efforts the Holy Spirit made to turn people from that type of life. We will find that some literally trod the Son of God underfoot, as they resisted His will while living their sinful and backslidden lives.

> That child of God soon begins to resist the leading of the Holy Spirit.

If God disqualified Moses for striking the rock (representing Christ and the sufficiency of His blood) instead of speaking to the rock, then we will see that countless Christians have counted the blood of Christ an unholy thing by the way they live. Actions speak louder than words.

Most children of God have in some way treated the Holy Spirit in a despiteful way by resisting, quenching, or grieving the Holy Spirit at some point in their lives.

Verse 30: "For we know him," – speaking to the saved.

Verse 31: "It is a fearful thing," – still speaking to the saved.

If you don't believe it is a fearful thing to fall into the hands of a living God, just ask King David, who received severe punishment. Ask Moses, whose ministry was cut short. Ask Nebuchadnezzar, who lived like an animal for seven years. Ask Achan or Ananias or Sapphira, who all died.

Verses 32-39: All of these verses are clearly speaking to the saved.

What Could Be Worse Than Death?

Again, why not ask King David what could possibly be worse than death? If this was possible, then King David would surely weep as he told you. David had at least two sons die. When you look at the contrast of David's reactions toward the deaths of these two sons, you can see clearly **what could be worse than death**.

Before his baby boy died, David fasted and prayed for days. After the baby died, he got up, bathed, worshipped God, and then ate dinner.

His servants inquired why he was so calm after all of his praying and tears. David simply answered, "**I cannot bring him back, but I can go to where he is.** He is in paradise and I will see him again." II Sam 12:21-23

Contrast that with the weeping and screaming when Absalom was killed. David screamed, "0 my son Absalom, my son, my son Absalom! Would God **I had died for thee,** O Absalom, my son, my son!" II Sam 18:33

Why all the screaming and uncontrollable bereavement? David was screaming because Absalom was in hell, and his blood was on David's hands. Absalom was never saved. **For David, it was worse than death.**

There will be thousands of rebellious parents who will live with the memories of what their wicked, self-centered lives have done to their families, and to others for the entire 1000 years.

> Why all the screaming and uncontrollable bereavement? David was screaming because Absalom was in hell and his blood was on David's hands.

Some in sympathy will exclaim, "How awful! How terrible!"

Wait! Please wait and think a minute. What about the victims **who are suffering in hell because of the sinful lives of their backslidden parents?**

- They walked all over Jesus by their sinful lives.
- They brought reproach to the precious blood of Christ by their sinful lives.
- They did respite to and resisted the Holy Spirit by their sinful lives.
- God was active in these backsliders' lives.

He offered them grace. But now, "…he shall have judgment without mercy, that hath showed no mercy…." James 2:13

Somewhere in the position of servitude, these people will serve for 1000 years in a state that they would give anything to change, but it is too late. They denied God's grace over and over again and now they must brace up and live in the judgment that their sinful lives have dictated. Some parents will face something worse than death for 1000 years.

THE NIGHTMARES THAT SOME PARENTS WILL LIVE WITH

What exactly will they dread and lament about? What could be

> Somewhere in the position of servitude, these people will serve for 1000 years in a state that they would give anything to change, but it is too late.

worse than death? Some of their children will be in hell. They will have to witness their eternal banishment. They will have to live with the regrets of their wasted life. Oh, the lonely, agonizing days that will drag by throughout the 1000 years! They would gladly die, if they could only go back and change things.

In the next section, we will examine those **parent's lifestyles that** will cause them to live through the full Millennial Reign with **something worse than death.**

SOME PARENTS WHO FAIL TO PROPERLY USE GOD'S BLESSINGS WILL BRING ABOUT SOMETHING WORSE THAN DEATH

There are two common practices that will bring parents to the place of living 1000 years with something **worse than death.** These two mistakes are so **human and natural** for parents to make that it took the wisdom of the wisest man who ever lived to expose them.

SOLOMON REFERRED TO THESE PRACTICES AS SORE EVILS

The information concerning these

human mistakes comes from the book of *Ecclesiastes*; the book that God commissioned Solomon to write to reveal **man's purpose on this earth.** This book also reveals how man can be happy and have tremendous satisfaction with his life.

When Solomon said that something was bad or empty, he used the word "*vanity.*" If it was a stage of evil, more than vanity, he used "*vanity of vanities,*" meaning that the deed was very sinful and empty. But if it was something worse than very sinful, he used the term "**sore evil**," which meant it was worse than death. He used this tern, "sore evil," twice in the book of Ecclesiastes.

If one reads the book of Ecclesiastes, he will discover that it is a series of experiments by King Solomon to discover why man was placed on the earth. After each experiment, he would declare that that type of life was not the lifestyle that man was created to live. Some the experiments Solomon tried were:

- **The lunacy of liquor** or the emptiness and foolishness of alcohol – Ecclesiastes 2:1-3;Proverbs 23:29-35

- **The ludicrousness of laughter** or living it up –Ecclesiastes 2:1-3; Ecclesiastes 7:6
- **The lucid emptiness of luxury** or the fruition of what money can buy- Ecclesiastes 2:4-11
- **The laborious worriment of labor** or who's going to get what I leave behind- Ecclesiastes 2:16-20
- **The lying of lust** or deceived to despair- Ecclesiastes 2:1-12

After each experiment, Solomon maintained that man was placed on this earth for a far greater purpose than what he found from living in that realm. After each experiment, he would express sadness and emptiness; and declared *"vanity, all is vanity."*

Every scientific experiment demands a conclusion. The wisest man on earth gave his findings in *Ecclesiastes 12:13-14*. In his summary, he gave the general purpose for man's existence on the earth. His deductions, after a lifetime of

> "Fear God, and keep his commandments: for this is the whole duty of man. For God shall bring every work unto judgment, with every secret thing, whether it be good, or whether it be evil."

investigation into God's purpose for creating man and the reason He placed him on the earth, are very pointed. Memorize Solomon's inspired to discover why you and the rest of the human race are alive. Solomon stated, "Let us hear the conclusion of the whole matter: Fear God, and keep his commandments: for this is the whole duty of man. For God shall bring every work unto judgment, with every secret thing, whether it be good, or whether it be evil." Ecc 12:13-14

The First Sore Evil Is Money Kept To One's Own Hurt

"There is a sore evil which I have seen under the sun, namely, riches kept for the owners thereof to their hurt." Ecc 5:13

This does not sound like a serious offense on the surface; something done with money that will cause one to face something **worse than death for 1000 years.**

"You must be kidding!" remarks one reader. "No," responds another, "He sounds like one of those money hungry preachers you see on television." Please! Before you jump to any conclusions, consider how God looks at the whole matter. **The Bible boldly claims that the earth is the Lord's and the fullness thereof.** It is His by right of creation, by right of His maintenance, and by right of His redemption. He bought it back from destruction by His death on Calvary.

The Bible teaches that a person's role on earth is **not one of ownership, but one of stewardship.** The Bible also teaches that God gives people different abilities or talents to be used **for their welfare and God's glory.** Paul stated this truth when he wrote, "Having then differing according to the

> He *was* quickly asked, "Where did you get the strength to work? Where did you get the brain to think and plan?"

grace that is given to its..." Rom 12:6 Paul continued on by naming the various gifts that God gives His children. In verse eight, he states that making money is one of these gifts. Paul admonished those that have the gift of making money, "he that giveth, let him do it with simplicity [liberally]."

Solomon stated that God gives man "riches, wealth and honor." Ecc 6:2 One man rebelled at the statement that God gave him riches and wealth. He said, "God hasn't given me anything! I've worked for everything I ever got!"

He was quickly asked, "Where did you get the strength to work? Where did you get the brain to think and plan?" The ungrateful man quickly dropped his head and left the area.

Please consider these sequences of events when one keeps money to his own hurt:
- God gives a man talent to make money.
- God blesses that talent.
- God adds His blessing in order for that man to use his money to bless or help others.
- The man keeps the money to his own hurt by hoarding up the money he doesn't even need.
- Therefore, God's **purpose for blessing** the man's talent goes unfulfilled.
- The need that people had, that God blessed the man with money to supply, **is never satisfied.**
- The people **perish.**
- The money **gathers mildew** in the bank.

- The man who earned the money inwardly **dries up** and becomes hardened and bitter.
- **Everyone is a loser,** the man kept the money that God gave him to bless humanity, **to his own hurt.**
- At the Judgment Seat of Christ, the man faces the truth, the reason God **gave him the money.** That it was not his own to use for self-gratification, but it was given by God to bless other people. He sees what **God intended** to be done, that was not done. The missionary that **was starved** off the field. The souls that the missionary would have won are languishing **in hell.**

Through his act of hoarding money, the numbers of souls suffering are multiplied. It is like a domino effect, one soul influencing another, which causes many to be lost in hell. The overall affect of **hoarding money is the reason Solomon calls it a "sore evil"** (something worse than death), and describes the person that kept the blessing of making money **to his own hurt** a "sore evil."

SOME PARENTS' BLESSINGS WILL TURN INTO A CURSE (SOMETHING WORSE THAN DEATH)

- God blesses a man with talent to **build a prosperous business.**
- The man has a son that he programs to take over and **expand the business.**
- From a child the son **works in the family business** after school, on weekends, and during summer vacations.
- The father sends the son to college to study and **prepare to run** the business.
- The son understands and accepts his role to push the business and the family name **to greater heights.**
- The son catches the vision and spirit of building the business and **works enthusiastically.**
- **Everything in the son's life** is programmed to improve and build the business.

- The company **goes public** and its stock soars.
- This **growth goes on** for a lifetime and the company becomes well known.

THEN, SOMETHING WORSE THAN DEATH HAPPENS. Listen to the summation of the **father and mother who programmed** their son to run the family business. This was their "little darling." They were going to make him **affluent, well known,** and enable him to **live with prestige and honor.** Everything they did was for **his welfare and happiness.** But God reveals the tragedy of it all, through Solomon, who spoke of the son in this light – the son is born **with "...nothing in his hand."** Ecc 5:14 "As he came, forth of his mother's womb, **naked shall he return to go as he came, and shall take nothing of his labour,** which he may carry away in his hand." Ecc 5:15

> He was addicted to the business. All of his life, goals, and thoughts were of the business, and God calls what he did for a full lifetime, **"laboring for the wind!"**

Solomon's summation is in verse 16, that for all of his work in building the business, all of his dedication, and long hours of labor for the family name, his paycheck was as if, **"HE HATH LABORED FOR THE WIND."** He was addicted to the business. All of his life, goals, and thoughts were of the business, and God calls what he did for a full lifetime, **"laboring for the wind!"**

How tragic! And his father and mother **did it to him!** It almost causes me to weep to think about it. Words will not describe the pain and emptiness of this whole ordeal.

BUT THAT IS NOT HALF OF THE HEARTACHE AND TRAGEDY

The Bible states in *verse 17,* that because of his sickness (addiction to the company), he laid down in **darkness. He died and went to hell.**

> Mom and dad programmed their own son to **labor for the wind,** and then die and go to hell. He worked like a slave, only to leave it all and lie down in darkness.

Mom and dad programmed their own son to **labor for the wind,** and then die and go to hell. He worked like a slave, only to leave it all and lie down in darkness.

You haven't heard the worst part yet! His influence and life caused many of his family members and acquaintances to follow in his footsteps.

But the "**something worse than death**" comes in at the Judgment Seat, where the parents have to face what **they did** to their little darling who trusted them.

They will live in a place of servitude, remembering what they did to their children and grandchildren, for a full 1000 years – **something worse than death.**

No wonder Solomon's description of this tragic story was **"a very sore evil under the sun."**

> They will live in a place of servitude, remembering what they did to their children and grandchildren, for a full 1000 years – **something worse than death.**

Chapter Nine
THOSE WHO WILL SHED TEARS IN THE KINGDOM PART B

One of the most honored positions in the world is that of a pastor. God has never done anything greater for a man than to hand pick him to stand before his people, to

> God offers grace for every occasion, power to do every work, and promises to never leave him or forsake him.

preach and teach the eternal, infallible Word of God. He has the closest relationship with God, as God directs him to care for His flock. God offers grace for every occasion, power to do every work, and promises to never leave him or forsake him. God shows absolute trust in him and **will reward him with glory that fadeth not away** if he is faithful to God's sacred trust. There is nothing like being one of God's preachers.

> But woe to the unfaithful pastor, who begins to be self-centered and self sufficient and misuses his sacred trust and office.

The prophet, pastor, preacher, minister, or chosen man of God has always been counted as the highest calling, or office, that a man could fill. It is a man whom God has chosen as an under-shepherd, who serves as God's spokesman. All true preachers have been chosen, or called, by God.

But woe to the unfaithful pastor, who begins to be self-centered and self sufficient and misuses his sacred trust and office.

THE PREACHER WHO WILL PLOW 1000 YEARS

"And strangers shall stand and feed your flocks, and the sons of the alien shall be your plowmen and your vinedressers." Isaiah 61:5

THE WORK AND ROLE OF A PASTOR

The apostle Peter told pastors to feed the flock (church of God). They were to take the leadership of the local church, not by constraints, but with a willing mind. Their motive for shepherding and feeding the spiritual sheep was not for money or prestige. They were to lead by example and be a role

> They were to lead by example and be a role model for Christian men, which will bring them conflict and hardship.

model for Christian men, which will bring them conflict and hardship. Many of the members will not submit themselves to God and His instruction. They will rebel against God's Word and **focus their rebellion toward the man of God.** We see this in the life of Moses in the Old Testament and the apostle Paul in the New Testament.

A RICH PAY DAY WAS OFFERED TO FAITHFUL PASTORS

Peter spoke of God's payday for His preachers, as servant leaders. In *I Peter 5:10,* Peter said that the God of all grace, who had called them (pastors) to share His (Christ's) eternal glory after they had suffered a while, would make them good settled leaders. Please note that **He called them to share in His eternal glory**. Peter said in verse 4 that the glory He promised is a "glory which fadeth not away."

> If he is faithful in his ministry, God promises him a reward in the 1000-year reign.

So a pastor is to stand for and teach spiritual things as God instructs him to teach. His lifestyle is one of a role model and servant leader. He is to see that things are done according to the Bible, knowing that it will cause him some opposition and personal problems. If he is faithful in his ministry, God promises him a reward in the 1000-year reign.

REWARDS FOR GOOD PASTORS, PUNISHMENT FOR BAD

In Luke 12:35-48, Jesus instructed the apostles about His imminent return and the rewards or punishments that preachers will receive at that time.

First, He said to watch (for His second coming) because they know not when He may return. "Be ye therefore ready also: for the Son of man cometh at an hour when ye think not." verse 40

Peter then asked the Lord, "Are you speaking to everyone or to pastors particularly?" verse 41

Jesus answered Peter by asking him a question. "...Who then is that faithful and wise steward, whom his lord shall make ruler over his household, to give them their portion [feed the flock] of meat in due season?" verse 42

Then Jesus promised that those who were faithful would be rewarded by the Lord when He comes back. In verse 43, He said, "Blessed is that servant, whom his lord when he cometh shall find so doing."

Jesus then turned His attention to pastors who have lost their focus and vision, and **say in their heart, "my Lord delayeth His coming**." They do not believe that Jesus is coming back any time soon, so they begin to take too much authority upon themselves, which leads to the mistreatment of some of the members. The pastors begin to beat or abuse some of the flock. They become drunk with their authority and position that the Lord entrusted them with.

> The pastors begin to beat or abuse some of the flock. The pastors become drunken by their authority and the position with which the Lord had entrusted them.

When the Lord comes back, He catches the abusive pastors unaware. In verse 46 the Bible states, He "...will cut him in sunder [cut him down to size] and will appoint him, **his portion with the unbelievers.**"

Their portion will be to work with the unbelievers who are plowing or taking care of the vineyards in the 1000-year reign.

In chapter three we showed there will be millions of people from the sheep nations which will be transferred into the millennium in there natural bodies. Most of those people were lost.

Throughout the 1000 year reign most of those sinners will accept Christ and be saved. In Isaiah 61:4-5 it talks of the labor force which will work in the millennium. It states that the "Sons of alien shall be your plowman and your vinedressers" some of these laborers are unsaved. Jesus will banish the unfaithful pastors to work with these sinners.

The proud and lofty pastors, who took too much authority, forgot about the second coming of the Lord. Instead of sharing in His eternal glory, these pastors will be appointed lowly servant jobs working in the labor gang with some of those who wasted their lives. **Some preachers will weep and plow for 1000 years**. They will have to face those they should have won to Christ at the Great White Throne Judgment and witness as

> They will see the lost cast into hell, and weep because they exalted themselves as a pastor monarch instead of a servant leader.

they are cast into the Lake of Fire.

Every morning, as they plow, they will remember what they did. They will remember how they betrayed their sacred trust and the calling of the Lord. They will try not to think about the future. Each time they remember their horrible appointment at the Great White Throne Judgment, they do so with a dread that haunts them. They will see the lost cast into hell and weep because they exalted themselves as a pastor monarch instead of a servant leader.

Their only comfort will come from the promise that God will wipe away all their tears before He takes them to the eternal Heaven. Their relief will take place only when their loving Father causes all of the former things to be forgotten. Rev 21:4

Until then, they will plow on in dread and tears. They will long to get the 1000 years over with, but another part of them will hope it never comes to an end. This is because they will then have to experience the ordeal at the Great White Throne

> They begin to like to plow and work hard because that is the only thing that takes their mind off of the consequences of a wasted ministry and life.

Judgment before they will ever have peace again.

What a high price the sin of pride has cost them. They begin to like to plow and work hard because that is the only thing that takes their mind off the consequences of a wasted ministry and life. The teardrops fall as they plow for the 1000 years, waiting and longing to be brought back into fellowship with their Heavenly Father.

Remember, in the Scripture, God warns the pastor that God resists the proud, but gives grace to the humble. I Peter 5:5 He clearly states that the lofty (proud) will be brought low. The pastor, who lived and abused his office in this life, will weep as he works with the labor crew, plowing for a full 1000 years.

> But to weep and gnash your teeth out of fellowship with God reveals ultimate pain, and a person given over to utter loneliness.

Remember pastor! You preached it and the Bible teaches it. God will not be mocked. You will reap what you sow and it will be for the full Millennial Reign.

IT WILL BE WORSE THAN WHAT HAS BEEN STATED

Some will look at a pile of ashes that represents their life's work, and weep. Some will look upon the effects of their sinful life and weep. They have to bare something worse than death. Some pastors who broke their Master's sacred trust will plow one row after another, mile after mile, and weep.

But to weep and gnash your teeth out of fellowship with God reveals ultimate pain, and a person given over to utter loneliness. That is exactly the place our final example finds himself, as he faces his upcoming 1000 years on the earth.

A POISONOUS SERVANT CAST INTO OUTER DARKNESS

This is a very simple story. What makes it difficult is that most people **do not like the way it ends**. They do not like the judgment that the third servant receives.

A man called his three servants in and gave them certain sums of money according to their different abilities. They were to manage the money and increase it on his behalf while he was gone on a trip.

Two of these servants went to work and doubled their lord's money. The third servant dug a hole and put his lord's money in it for safekeeping, but did not do anything to increase it.

After a period of time, the master returned and called his three servants in to give an account of their stewardship.

The first two brought their sums of money and reported that they had doubled his original capital. Their lord said the same words to both of the servants and rewarded each of them.

The third servant went and dug up his lord's money and gave it back to him, and used some uncomplimentary words while doing so. His lord stripped him of what he had given him, then rebuked him and punished him. This, to some, is a very harsh judgment. Therefore it is difficult for them to accept the plain teaching that some of God's children, who backslide and live a rebellious life that turns many sinners away from Christ, will face severe punishment at the Judgment Seat.

> The third servant went and dug up his lord's money and gave it back to him, and used some uncomplimentary words while doing so.

Matthew, Chapter 25, points out the severity with which God will judge the backslidden children who harbor bitterness.

MATTHEW CHAPTER 25, DEPICTS THREE DIFFERENT JUDGMENTS

The 25th Chapter of Matthew reveals the judgments that will take place at the second coming of Jesus Christ.

The Bible teaches that Jesus will come back to reward His faithful servants, and execute righteous judgment. One of Jesus' last promises, before returning to Heaven, was, "...behold, I come quickly; and my reward is with me, to give every man according as his work shall be." Rev 22:12

> There are three distinct judgments dealt with in Matthew, chapter 25.

The second coming of Jesus will be in two phases. He will come for His saints before the Tribulation period, and then seven years later (less a few days), He will come back to the earth with His saints. There are three distinct judgments dealt with in Matthew, Chapter 25.

Matthew 25:1-13, **deals with the judgment of institutions, or churches.**

> The judgment of individual Christians will reveal their works as a Christian while on the earth. Each Christian must give an account of his works, whether they are good or bad.

Matthew 25:14-30, deals with the **judgment of individual Christians.** Both of these judgments take place before the Tribulation period.

Matthew 25:31-46, deals with the judgment of nations, which will take place at the end of the 7-year tribulation, when Jesus comes back in glory with His holy angels.

The Judgment of churches reveals that what a church believes and practices is very important. Each individual member will be rewarded or punished for what his church did and taught.

The judgment of individual Christians will reveal their works as a Christian while on the earth. **Each Christian must give an account** of his works, whether they are good or bad.

The judgment of nations reveals the responsibility each citizen has in supporting Biblical principles in his own country. Christians will be rewarded or punished based on what their country has done.

These three different judgments show the responsibility of a person **as a church member, as an individual, and as a citizen of his country.** They also show that we will have to stand in judgment and be rewarded or punished based on our works on earth. We are not our own. We have been bought with a price. Therefore, **our proper roll on earth is as stewards of Christ**. At His second coming, we must give a complete account of all phases of our life.

JUDGMENT OF INDIVIDUAL STEWARDSHIP

The purpose of the story in Matt 25:14-30, is to show that each person will stand personally and individually before his Lord and give account of his stewardship and life. He will be dealt with in direct proportion to his life works and attitude. The setting of the encounter will be at the Judgment Seat of Christ, where judgment of individual stewardship will take place.

> At His second coming, we must give a complete account of all phases of our life.

In order to determine the truths that Jesus is teaching, we will study the words used, along with the attitudes of the four principals in this story.

Study of the Word Usage for the Word "Servant"

The usage of the word "servant" or

"servants" is dealt with in the following verses:

Verse 14: The story begins with a man calling **his own servants**. Together, there is no distinction made concerning what type of servants they were. The distinction made, concerns the different degrees of their natural capabilities.

Verse 19: After a long period of time, the man, called "the lord of those servants," comes back to check on the three concerning their individual **stewardship.**

Verse 21: "Well done, thou good and faithful servant," was the commendation the man made to the first servant.

Verse 23: "Well done, thou good and faithful servant," was the commendation the man made to the second servant.

Verse 26: "Thou wicked and slothful servant," was the rebuke of the man to the third servant.

Verse 30: "cast ye the unprofitable servant into outer darkness," was the punishment meted out to the third servant.

> The word "servant" is used by the lord describing these three men *six times,* and is the same word and means the same thing in all six places.

The word "servant" is used by the lord describing these three men **six *times,*** and is the same word and means the same thing in all six places. The meaning of the word "servant" is "child of God." If one of them was a servant, then all of them were servants. If one of them was a child of God, then all three of them were children of God.

The use of the word "servant" will not allow a different interpretation, one to one servant and another to another servant. The word usage dictates that all three servants were saved and belonged to the owner and were accountable to him.

Study of the Word Usage for the Word, "Lord"

The usage of the word, "lord," is dealt with in the following verses:

Verse 18: The third servant "hid his lord's money." The servant hid the money he had been entrusted with to use for his **lord's benefit and good.**

Verse 19: "After a longtime, the lord of those servants cometh," to find out how each of his three servants had obeyed his command of using their talent for their master's well being and good.

Verses 22 and 24: The two obedient

servants came and **both happily presented** their gain to their lord.

Verses 21, 23 and 26: All three of these verses begin with the same expression, "his **lord said unto him.**" He referred to all three of his servants in the same way. It is clear by the word usage that all three were his servants.

> *Verses 21, 23 and 26*: All three of these verses begin with the same expression, *"his **lord said unto** him."*

Verses 24 and 30: The disobedient servant addressed the man as "lord," and when the lord cast him out of his sight, his lord called him an **"unprofitable servant."** There is no change in position or in the way the lord dealt with him. The only difference is that two of his servants were obedient, **while the third was disobedient.**

If the use of the word "servant" means "child of God," then the use of the words "lord" or "his lord" must mean our Lord, Jesus Christ. The study of the usage of these words clearly proves that they were individual children of God at the Judgment Seat, being judged for their individual stewardship.

Study of Attitudes Manifested

There are several different attitudes manifested within this chapter. Let us look at each of them.

The Obedient and Faithful Servants

Two of the servants had good, obedient attitudes. When they received their stewardship, they **immediately** went to work and doubled the gift which their lord had committed to their trust.

> When the lord returned, he found the first two servants busy working on his behalf.

- **They were obedient.** When the lord returned, he found the first two servants busy working on his behalf.
- **They were faithful.** Both the first and the second servants came and happily presented the gains of their faithful stewardship.
- **They were rewarded.** The lord commended each servant, "thou has been faithful over a, few things, 1 will make thee ruler over many things: enter thou into the joy of thy lord."

The Disobedient and Unfaithful Servant

The third servant was bitter and willfully disobedient. As soon as he was given the money to work with, he deliberately disobeyed his lord and hid it.

- **He was willfully disobedient**. He hid his talent. He took it from the lord, and hid it immediately. He never even tried to be obedient.
- **He was unthankful**. His lord gave him his talent and the opportunity to serve him. There is not one sign of gratitude from the servant. In fact, the opposite is true. **He manifested bitterness and anger toward his lord**. When he came into his lord's presence, he instantly accused him of being a harsh and uncaring man. He further accused him of taking advantage of other people's property and personal rights. This accusation toward the lord **showed a long standing anger and bitterness** that he harbored against his lord for a long time.
- **He was fearful and unbelieving**. This servant tried to justify his rebellious behavior by saying that he

was afraid. Fear is the opposite of faith. The servant may have been fearful of what others might think or say about him. He may have been afraid of failing. Regardless of what he was fearful of, it led him to live a life of unbelief and disobedience.
- **He had a blameful spirit**. "It wasn't me lord. It was you! You were so harsh. You reaped where you hadn't sowed. I would have worked, but you were such a bully. I was afraid to try," was the implication of his defense.
- **He was lazy**. How do we know he was lazy? His lord, who knew his heart and actions, called him a wicked and slothful (lazy) servant.

To be absent from the body is to be present with the Lord. Nothing changes in a person's relationship with the Lord when they die, **except location**. Here, the servant disobeyed his lord from the beginning. He lived a lifetime of disobedience and laziness, and manifested a bitter, hateful spirit against his lord. **He manifested the same attitude** at the Judgment Seat **that he had been manifesting during his life.**

When a saved person backslides, God chastises him in order to correct him and save his life of service. **One of two things happens** when God chastises

> He lived a lifetime of disobedience and laziness and manifested a bitter, hateful spirit against his lord. He manifested the same attitude at the Judgment Seat that he had been manifesting during his life.

one of His children. The child of God either repents and turns back to serve the Lord, or he resents the chastisement and becomes more hardened. God chastises him again. And again, a child of God **both repents and turns back** to the service of the Lord, **or he becomes more resentful and hard.** Soon, unless he repents, the **child of God turns bitter and begins to accuse God.** The third servant was this type of person. When his lord gave him his talent and commanded him to go to work, **he refused instantly** and hid his lord's money.

STUDY THE PHRASE, THE LORD OF THE SERVANTS

The lord gave all three servants life, opportunity, and a chance to

> The third servant refused to work, rebelled, and came to the Judgment Seat **with a rebellious, hateful attitude.**

excel and build for the future. Two of them took advantage of his goodness and served well in their stewardship and were rewarded. The third servant refused to work, rebelled, and came to the Judgment Seat **with a rebellious, hateful attitude.** When his lord asked him to give an account of his stewardship, he blamed his lord for his failures.

What is God going to do? God gave us life. He redeemed us from a horrible condemnation and lost eternity by sending His Son to die in our place so we could be saved. He gave us an opportunity to live a life in his good, acceptable and perfect will.

> He would not respond to God's gentle chastisement and correction in his life. He would not turn, regardless of how his Heavenly Father tried to help him.

Is He going to let us get away with it by throwing a temper tantrum? We are not dealing with a modern, weak-kneed set of parents who have a worldly sentiment of raising children. We are dealing with the sovereign King of Heaven. This rebellious, hard-headed, strong-willed child of His had been bullying people as he lived his wicked and slothful life for a long time. He would not respond to God's gentle chastisement and correction in his life. He would not turn, regardless of how his Heavenly Father tried to help him.

Now it is judgment time, "Thou slothful and wicked kid. Sit down now and listen. You are at the bar of justice, not a bargaining table; and it is now time for you to give an account of your life."

> God gave each person life, opportunity and talent. He did this for our good and for God's glory.

Study of Judgment Rendered

The following instructions were given regarding the judgment and punishment of the unfaithful servant.

Take from him the sum of money. "It is not his, it is mine. I gave it to him to use, and since he didn't use it, I'm taking it back and giving it to someone who will." God gave each person life, opportunity, and talent. He did this for our good and for God's glory. In this story, there is a clear understanding that it was the lord's money and that the three men were his servants. There will be a day, in the future, when the boss will have his servants give an account of their stewardship. Their lord gave it to them to use. If they did not use it wisely, it was still his to take back and give to someone who would use it wisely.

Cast him into outer darkness. The Lord didn't say, "Cast him into hell." Jesus knows the difference between outer darkness and hell. Later in this very chapter, Jesus commands the angels to throw the goat nations into hell. (Matthew 25:41) If He meant for them to cast this servant into hell, then he would have surely said so. He said, **"cast him into outer darkness."** Again, these three men represent three men who were servants, or **who were saved,** but these men were owned by the lord, who had given them talents to use for his benefit. They were required to give an account of their stewardship. They would be rewarded if they worked, but they would suffer loss if they did not work.

Darkness is a symbol of being out of the presence and fellowship of the ruler.

> Darkness is a symbol of being out of the presence and fellowship of the ruler.

In Biblical days, a reception or dinner was given to honor a certain official or royalty. Since they had a lighting problem, the guest with the highest degree of importance and honor was always seated in closest to the light. People of lesser rank were relegated to areas of lesser light. Others were invited who stood in the edge of light. Those **who were not favored** with the host were **kept in the outer darkness,** which showed their standing with the person in charge.

Study of The Word Usage For The Words "Light" And "Darkness"

"And have **no fellowship** with the unfruitful **works of darkness,** but rather reprove them." Eph 5:11

> *"And have **no fellowship** with the unfruitful **works of darkness,** but rather reprove them.*

"But if we walk **in the light,** as he is in the light, **we have fellowship** one with another...." I .John 1:7

"If we say that we have **fellowship** with him [Christ], and **walk in darkness,** we lie, and do **not the truth."** I John 1:6

The usage of the words "light" and "darkness", plus the traditions of the day in which this event happened, teaches that outer darkness is referring to the position a person assumed because of his unfaithfulness and attitude.

Outer darkness means out of fellowship. The rebellious servant was cast out of fellowship with his Lord for 1000 years.

> The usage of the words "light" and "darkness", plus the traditions of the day in which this event happened, teaches that outer darkness is referring to the position a person assumed because of his unfaithfulness and attitude.

- **He will get out of bed** every day for 1000 years, with the knowledge that he wasted his life as he serves somewhere on the earth in a servant status
- **He will relive** the Judgment Seat scene in his mind for 1000 years.
- **He will dread having to witness** the Great White Throne Judgment for 1000 years.
- **He will weep** for 1000 years.
- **He will gnash** his teeth in pain for 1000 years, as he suffers the consequences of a life lived in rebellion and slothfulness.

> **He will gnash** his teeth in pain for 1000 years, as he suffers the consequences of a life lived in rebellion and slothfulness.

When King Saul was cast out

of fellowship with God, **he almost lost his mind because of his loneliness.** This dear man will live and be out of fellowship with his Lord for a full 1000 years.

This is the way the King has of sending a message to others. "You cannot come into my throne room and accuse me of being harsh and uncaring, after I loved you enough to die for you. You are not going to come into my throne room before the royalty and angels of Heaven and **tell me that you knowingly and willfully did just the opposite** of what I personally told you to do; and then try to blame me for your slothful, wicked life!"

- I am the boss!
- I gave you life.
- I tried to bless you.
- I tried to turn you.
- I will not accept any blame for your wasted life.
- I loved you, died for you, and did everything in my power to help you."

"Take what I gave him, and get him out of here!

> Cast him out of fellowship. Let him go suffer the consequences of a wicked and slothful life for 1000 years.

Cast him out of fellowship. Let him go suffer the consequences of a wicked and slothful life for 1000 years. Let him get up every morning and remember those that were turned away from salvation by his bitter, slothful life. Let him feel the loneliness of being out of fellowship with his Lord, and cast him out of my presence for the full 1000 years!"

"He is still ten thousand times better off than those that he let go to hell. His punishment for his wicked and slothful life is to weep and gnash his teeth, out of divine fellowship, for 1000 years." Those who died and went to hell because of his self-centered and rebellious life will suffer in hell forever.

Can you see yourself in the role of one of these three servants? Perhaps a better question would be, where will you live during your 1000 years on the earth under the reign of King Jesus?

Chapter Ten
A PLEADING CALL TO THE ELEVENTH HOUR CHRISTIANS

In the latter stage of Jesus' earthly ministry, humanly speaking, He had a problem. The time for His offering of Himself upon the cross, His death, resurrection, and soon ascension back to Heaven, was at hand.

> "Are the apostles ready to assume the complete leadership of the worldwide effort to preach the Gospel to every creature?"

"Are the apostles ready to assume the complete leadership of the worldwide effort to preach the Gospel to every creature?"

John's and James' mother had just approached Him about her sons' roll in the coming Kingdom. Judas would betray Him for thirty pieces of silver. Thomas, although a very good man, had the tendency to doubt. In fact, all of the apostles were slow to grasp the spiritual truths that went against their traditions.

"Through the trauma of my death and the magnitude of the tasks I have given them, will they hold together? Or will the devil be able to inject enough doubt into their minds, coupled with their inferiority complexes, to cause the whole effort to go down the tubes?"

"I must do something to grab their attention, hypnotize their minds, and motivate them to give their all until their deaths. The whole world is lying in spiritual darkness, lost without God, condemned to spend eternity in hell; unless someone brings them the good news that, through my shed blood, there is remission of sins. But someone must go and tell them. These apostles are the ones that must lead this assault against the gates of hell."

"Are they up to it? Will they stay focused? Can they endure the pressure and persecution?"

The author knows that Jesus didn't think this way, because He was perfect God dwelling in human flesh, but He had a cause to do so.

WHAT IS THE SOLUTION?

Through the reading of this book, you have the answer. Offer them a personal fellowship with me (Jesus) for the full 1000 years in the Kingdom, as regional kings over the twelve tribes of Israel.

He offered them the positions and spent forty days drilling this promise into their heads before going back to Heaven.

> Offer them a personal fellowship with me (Jesus) for the full 1000 years in the Kingdom, as regional kings over the twelve tribes of Israel.

The apostles' minds and souls were completely absorbed with this idea. They were captured by this promise!

Now, as Paul Harvey would say, "You know the rest of the story!" The Gospel was carried throughout the world and millions were saved!

TODAY, JESUS HAS A BIGGER PROBLEM

The author is still humanly speaking, but Jesus has a bigger problem. It is a SIX AND ONE-HALF TO SEVEN BILLION times bigger problem. There are over six billion souls in the world today and most of them are lost.

THE PROBLEM ILLUSTRATED

The Crop Is Perishing. With the crop in the field, a storm brewing, and a shortage of workers, how can a farmer sleep, much less kick back and retire? Everything he has worked for all of his life hangs in the balance.

He whispers, "Oh God, give me the strength to labor on," as he throws every ounce of his energy into saving his crop. Jesus has six and one-half to seven billion souls in His harvest, and time is running out.

The Towers Are Down and People Are Dying. Terrorists have struck and the towers are down. Thousands are dead or trapped. Is it a time for a vacation; or is it a time for all out rescue?

> Jesus has six and one-half to seven billion souls in His harvest, and time is running out.

Can you hear the screams? Can you see the desperate faces? Can you assist the mangled? Can you feed the homeless? Is it a time for self-centeredness; or **is it a time for self-abasement**?

The city of New York responded. Mayor Guilliani thrust himself into the role of leadership. Men worked until they dropped. Other volunteers had to be physically restrained after hours of exhausted searching. They must find the trapped. They must save the dying.

Jesus has six and one-half to seven billion souls that will not only die, but they are facing eternal separation from God, in hell, forever.

GOD'S MOST PRECIOUS HARVEST IS PERISHING

God's most precious harvest of people is perishing. Jesus goes out into the vineyard and **THE SUN IS SINKING, THE TIME IS SHORT, and THE DAY IS FAR SPENT.**

Humanly speaking, the thoughts begin to rush through His mind. "Many of the magnificent creatures, my crowning creation, the ones I created to love and be loved by are lost. Multitudes upon multitudes, numbers beyond counting, are getting closer to death and eternal destruction. As sovereign Lord of the universe, **what shall I do**?"

"I have already sacrificed my Son on the cross for their reconciliation and salvation. I need workers, people to go and tell them of my provision. I need laborers to come and work in my vineyard and try to save the perishing souls."

"There are many standing idle! **Give a call**! SOUND THE ALARM! The day is ending! It is the Eleventh Hour! I need everyone, regardless of your experience or background. I don't care about past failures or a backslidden past. If you will throw your energy into this last ditch effort to save the harvest, I will pay you as if you worked **for me all day long**."

CAN I WORK THE SAME MAGIC AGAIN?

"The apostles were transformed from fishermen, or common workers, **into worldwide leaders**. Can I get my plan across to people living in the eleventh hour of this dispensation just before my second coming? There are billions of souls hanging in the balance. How can I motivate the people in the eleventh hour to throw themselves into the fields to save the perishing masses?"

> "There are many standing idle! **Give a call**! SOUND THE ALARM! The day is ending! It is the eleventh hour! I need anyone, everyone, regardless of your experience or background

Jesus said, "My sheep know my voice. If they have a clear understanding of what my voice (the Word of God) is saying, **they will respond**. Some how I must get my message **across to them, my urgent need of their help;** I will do this by drawing their attention to the event **that changed my apostles from unfocused men into fearless leaders**. Once I make this point clear to them and they can clearly see what transformed the apostles, I will make them the same offer of reward."

TRANSFORMING PRINCIPLES

The principle that Jesus revealed to the apostles in Matthew 19:27-30, **transformed them** from weak, discouraged preachers into powerful, fearless apostles. The apostles of average ability were transformed into fearless focused missionaries, which not only evangelized the major city of Jerusalem, but also were successful in getting the Gospel to the uttermost parts of the world in their **lifetime. Nothing in history can compare with the tremendous fervor and success of their ministries.**

A Brief Background of the Apostles' Thinking

The apostles had worked tirelessly for three and one-half years. Day and night, week after week, they had marveled and learned from their master teacher. The marvelous accomplishments and the huge crowds that had followed Jesus for three and one-half years **had dropped off until there were only a handful of followers** who attended the meetings. The apostles had forsaken all, and for three and one-half years they had traveled night and day with Jesus. **They were tired. They were becoming discouraged.**

Then something happened **that captivated their minds and held them spellbound** for the rest of their lives! They were never the same again. According to historians, this great revelation caused all of them except one, the apostle John, **to give their lives as martyrs** for the cause of their dear Lord. The lone exception, the apostle John, was still active for the Lord at the age of 93 when he penned the final book of the Bible, the *Book of Revelation*, from his place of exile on the isle of Patmos.

God's Will for The Eleventh Hour Christians

The foundation for this thought provoking story found *in Matthew 20:1-16,* is what transformed the apostles.

One must understand the principles found in this story in order to get the full impact of the second story.

We Are Talking About Rewards

Bear in mind that the subject matter in both stories **has to do with rewards.** Peter bluntly told the Lord, "We have forsaken all to follow you. What shall we have therefore?" **Simply stated – "What are you going to pay us for our sacrificial service?"**

The people in both stories were born again Christians, who had all been saved by the grace of God. They were saved because of the sacrificial payment that Jesus made on the Cross of Calvary. They are all going to heaven by His grace without any mixture of works or efforts on their part.

God Is Looking For the Same Transformation

No one can deny that the apostles were transformed. What principle or truth is it that God wants to use to transform the Christians who are living on the earth in this eleventh hour? In this chapter, we will learn what significance the eleventh hour has and why its message will have the same potential of transforming you, the reader, in the same way it transformed the apostles.

GOD'S CALL TO THE ELEVENTH HOUR CHRISTIANS

The author will give a verse by verse account of these stories with a few brief words of explanation. We will begin in Matthew 19:27.

Verse 27: "Then answered Peter and said unto him [Jesus], Behold, we have forsaken all, and followed thee: what shall we have therefore?"

> Jesus wanted him to ask the question to have the **opportunity of informing all of the apostles** of the great bonus or reward for their faithful service to Him.

If one would study the events recorded in the previous ten verses, you would see that Jesus provoked Peter into blurting out his startling question of, "What shall we have, therefore?"

Jesus wanted him to ask the question to have the **opportunity of informing all the apostles** of the great bonus or reward for their faithful service to Him.

Verse 28: "And Jesus said unto them [not just Peter alone], Verily, 1 say unto you [plural], That ye which have followed me, in the regeneration [new spiritual order] when the Son of man [referring to himself] shall sit in the throne of his glory [1000-year kingdom], ye also shall sit upon twelve thrones, judging the twelve tribes of Israel."

The Old Testament scriptures and the statement in the model prayer, "Thy Kingdom come," all point to a future Messianic Kingdom in which Jesus will sit upon King David's throne in the city of Jerusalem, and rule this earth in perfect peace for 1000 years.

Jesus said, in answer to Peter's question, "What is your paycheck for sacrificially serving me?" The answer, which changed the apostles' lives forever, was, "When I rule from Jerusalem, you twelve men will be in close proximity to me as you each rule over one of the twelve tribes of Israel for the same 1000 years."

The record of this promise, as recorded in Luke 22:30, makes it so pointed and clear. "That ye may eat and drink at my table in my kingdom, and sit on thrones judging the twelve tribes of Israel."

The condition for receiving the fulfillment of this promise was, "If you will faithfully serve me for the rest of your lives, then I will let you rule the earth with me for 1000 years." A position of honor which elevated them to the same level as Abraham, Israel, Moses, Elijah, and the rest of their heroes - for a full 1000 years and beyond. What a paycheck!

Authors Note: Jesus spent forty days expounding on this point just before he ascended back into heaven. Acts 1:3

Verse 29: "And every one that hath forsaken houses, or brethren, or sisters, or father, or mother, or wife, or children, or lands, for my name's sake, shall receive an hundredfold, and shall inherit everlasting life."

After stating this promise to the twelve apostles, Jesus turned to the **people of future generations.** Now, keep in mind the subject under consideration is **rewards,** not personal salvation from Hell.

The gift of God is eternal life. One cannot work for a gift. If he does, then it is no longer a free gift. We **do not inherit** everlasting life because it is a free gift, but we can inherit a hundred fold that will last forever, a reward.

Jesus is offering a paycheck, or reward, to the future followers who give up everything to follow Him - a reward which will bring **a hundred fold return** on their investments, which will be unto everlasting, or endless, life. **What a paycheck!**

Verse 30: "But many that are first shall be last; and the last shall be first."

Again, the subject is a paycheck or **reward.** The scope of the reward covers the **whole dispensation from the time of Jesus' ministry on the earth until He returns** the second time to become earth's King.

The people living during the apostle's time would be considered as "the first;" the ones living just before he comes the second time will would be considered **"the last."**

Jesus is saying, many that are first (living in his day) will be last in paychecks or rewards, and the last (those who are alive when He comes back) will be **first in rewards** or paychecks.

With these startling principles in mind, may we continue our verse by verse study of the thought provoking story in Matthew 20:1-16.

Verse 1: "For the kingdom of heaven [work of God] is like unto a man that is a householder [owner] that went out early in the morning to hire laborers into his vineyard."

> Jesus is saying, many that are first (living in his day) will be last in paychecks or rewards and the last (those who are alive when He comes back) will be **first in rewards** or paychecks.

Jesus is using the illustration of an owner of a vineyard who is seeking workers to harvest his grapes before they ruin, **to explain the work of God.**

Verse 2: "And when he had agreed with the labourers for a penny a day, he sent them into the vineyard."

The word "penny" comes from a word that means "a day's pay." Let's use a modern day figure of one hundred dollars as the amount they agreed upon as the day's pay.

The owner asked the people looking for work, "Will you work in the vineyard for me this day for $100?" The workers said, "Yes sir, we will be glad to work for the day's pay of $100."

Verse 3: "And he [the owner] went out about the third hour [9:00 o'clock], and saw others standing idle in the market place."

Three hours later the owner approached other people who were also looking for work.

Verse 4: "And he said unto them; Go ye also into the vineyard, and whatsoever is right I will give you. And they went their way."

Those in the market place agreed to work for a fair wage and started work at 9:00 o'clock in the morning.

Verse 5: "Again he went out about the sixth [12:00 o'clock] and ninth hour [3:00 o'clock in the afternoon], and did likewise."

The owner hired additional workers at noon and again others at three o'clock to work in his vineyard.

Verse 6: "And about the eleventh hour [5:00 o'clock] he went out, and, found others standing idle, and saith unto them, why stand ye here all the day idle?"

At the Eleventh Hour, or when the day was almost over, the owner hired the final laborers to work in his vineyard. He seemed surprised that they had been standing idle all day.

Verse 7: "They say unto him, **because no man has hired us**. He saith unto them, Go ye also into the vineyard; and whatsoever is right that, shall you receive."

Upon the owner's inquiry of why they were standing idle, they replied, "Because no man has hired us." The owner commissioned them to go into the vineyard and work upon his promise to pay them whatever was right. They went to work for the final hour of the day.

Verse 8: "So when even [evening] was come, the lord of the vineyard saith unto his steward [overseer], Call the laborers, and give them their hire, beginning from the last unto the **first.**"

The day ends, and the superintendent is told to pay the workers. Now, **we have something very strange happen.** The superintendent is to pay the last employees, who have only worked for one hour, FIRST. The normal procedure is to show respect for seniority, and pay those employees who have worked longer for the company first, and then the ones who have only worked for a short time, last. But in this thought provoking story, **we have that order reversed.**

Verse 9: "And when they came that were hired about the eleventh hour, they received every man a penny."

Can you imagine the shock and the elation of those workers who had worked about an hour when the superintendent handed each one of them a hundred dollar bill. I am sure that there was shouting and leaping for joy. Others may have shed tears of unbelief. A hundred dollars, or a full day's pay, for working for only one hour! Unheard of! WHAT AN ATTENTION GETTER! Why would the owner do this? Pay the last workers first and give them a full day's pay?

Verse 10: "But when the first came, they supposed that they should have received more; and they likewise received every man a penny."

The expectation of those hired early in the morning came crashing down when they also received $100.

Verse 11: "And when they had received it, they murmured against the goodman of the house."

They voiced their disappointment by murmuring against the owner who is referred to as "the goodman" of the house.

Verse 12: "Saying, These last have wrought but one hour, and thou **host made them equal unto us**, which have borne the burden and heat of the day."

They said, "It is not fair," and humanly speaking, many would agree. "We worked all day for twelve grueling, hot hours; and they worked for only hour, and you paid us the same amount as you paid them! **It is not fair!**"

Verse 13: "But he answered one of them [the spokesman], and said, Friend, I do thee no wrong: didst thou agree with me for a penny?"

The goodman answered kindly by stating, "Didn't you agree this morning that $100 would be a fair and just wage?"

Verse 14: "Take that thine is, and go thy way: I will give unto this last, even as unto thee."

He continued by saying, "Take your agreed salary and go your way because I am paying the eleventh hour workers the same $100 that I have paid you."

Verse 15: "Is it not lawful for me to do what I will with mine own? Is thine eye evil, because I am good?" The dialogue ran something like this:

Owner: "Isn't it my money?"
Worker: "Yes, sir."
Owner: "Can't I spend my money the way I please?"
Worker: "Yes, sir."
Owner: "Didn't I pay you exactly what we agreed on this morning?"
Worker: "Yes, sir."
Owner: "Then what is your complaint?"
Worker: "No complaint, sir."
Owner: "Has your eye become evil, because I treated someone good?"
Worker: No answer.

Verse 16: "So the last shall be first, and the first last: for many be called, but few chosen."

In this verse, Jesus is referring back to the last four verses in Matthew Chapter 19, where He was discussing the apostles' paychecks for their successful service to Him.

As you can see, this is a very strange and thought provoking story. Pay the last workers first, and give them exactly as much as those who worked all day long. Strange indeed! What on earth does it mean?

Note the expression, "For many be called, but few chosen."

The "many called" are those who are part of the eleventh hour. They are the ones who are invited by the Lord to go to work in His vineyard. The "few chosen" are those who accepted His offer and went to work.

THE PURPOSE OF THIS THOUGHT PROVOKING STORY

A casual observer might agree with the complaining workers who worked through the heat of the day and received the exact same pay as those who had worked but one hour. This story is contrary to the way that a company normally pays its workers. Workers, who have been with a company longer, generally are given more consideration than the people with less seniority.

Without understanding the details and purpose of this story, the average person would agree or at least be sympathetic toward the people who had worked all day.

This story was told by Jesus to, undoubtedly, cause people to stop and think. It was told to provoke people to find the answers to the following questions.

- Who is the householder?
- What does the vineyard represent?
- Who are the laborers?
- What does the day from 6:00 a.m. to 6:00 p.m. mean?
- What is the key to understanding this story?
- What significance does the Eleventh Hour have?
- Why did he pay all workers the same wage?
- Why did he pay the last workers first?
- When will this payday take place?
- What is the purpose of the story?
- Who is this story directed to primarily?
- What does this strange story mean?

THIS THOUGHT PROVOKING STORY THOUGHT OUT

In order to understand this puzzling story you must consider the following answers to those questions.

The householder (landowner) represents God. "The earth is the Lord's and the fullness thereof...." Psalms 24:1

The vineyard represents the kingdom work of rescuing sinners who, when they perish, will be lost forever in hell.

The laborers represent Christians or soul-winners. They were harvesting the **fruit, which are people.**

The day beginning at 6:00 AM and closing at 6:00 PM represents the whole dispensation, beginning with Jesus' ministry until the close of the age at His second coming.

The key to understanding their story is to interpret it within its setting. This story is part of the discussion that started in Matthew 19:27-30, which is dealing with rewards. The term "the last shall be first" in the previous story is clearly dealing with the whole church age, beginning with the apostles (the first) until the end of the age (the last), and the rewards that people will earn at the second coming of Christ.

The proper understanding of the Eleventh Hour is the heart of the story. The Eleventh Hour represents a period of time, WHICH IS VERY CLOSE TO THE END OF THE DAY, OR AGE. The Eleventh Hour, before His second coming, represents the ones who are alive when He returns. The Eleventh Hour also represents people who are saved during the latter time, or in the Eleventh Hour of their life.

Why did he pay all workers the same wage? He did this to motivate those who are alive now, in this Eleventh Hour period, realize **the great opportunity of our day**. Jesus, the Lord of the Harvest, is sending

> The proper understanding of the Eleventh Hour is the heart of the story. The Eleventh Hour represents a period of time, WHICH IS VERY CLOSE TO THE END OF THE DAY, OR AGE

this message, "If you will forget about everything that is going on all around you and really go to work to win souls in my vineyard for the one hour you have left, **then I will blot out all your past sins and pay you as if you worked your whole life for me.**"

Why did He pay the last workers first? He paid the last first in order to get your attention and to motivate you in this Eleventh Hour to get to work.

When is this payday? The answer to this question is found in Matthew 19:28. Jesus told the apostles that when He came back and started His Millennial Kingdom of

> **Why did He pay the last workers first?** He paid the last first in order to get your attention and to motivate you in this Eleventh Hour to get to work.

1000 years on this earth, they also would rule over the twelve tribes of Israel. The pay or reward for the Eleventh Hour Christians will be to work under King Jesus as one of His kings **during His glorious rule of 1000 years**

What is the purpose of this story? With this story, Jesus is attempting to enlist workers to become laborers for Him in this Eleventh Hour right before His second coming.

Who is Jesus directing this story to, primarily? There are three classes of people who are all alive on this earth at this very moment. The three classes of people could be three different groups of people or **all three could be found in the same group**.

Anyone who is saved in this period of time, in the waning moments before Jesus comes back.

Those who, according to their biological clock of sixty plus years, are in their Eleventh Hour. Many of these seniors and retired people could go

> **What is the purpose of this story?** With this story, Jesus is attempting to enlist workers to become laborers for Him in this Eleventh Hour right before His second coming.

full time in assisting in the Lord's work or in winning souls.

Those who are saved but who have been standing idle all their lives. There are many who go through some tragedy or have made dumb decisions that have shipwrecked their lives. The devil has made them think that God cannot or would not ever be able to use them again. This Eleventh Hour call from the Lord of the Harvest is saying, "Don't listen to the voices that keep you inactive. I need you! Souls are dying! Come on and help me and I will pay you like you have worked for me all of your life!"

What does this story mean? It means the need for workers is urgent. It means that the perishing soul, who is facing a Christless world, has only a short time in which to be saved. It means God is trying to speak to senior citizens and those who have made shipwrecks of their lives, that they are important and that he needs them. With this story, He is trying to reveal to them their real purpose in this day and age, and of His despair. He is calling them to enter the work of giving their lives and talents to His work of winning and training lost souls.

SPOTLIGHT THE PUNCH LINE IN THIS THOUGHT PROVOKING STORY

There is nothing worse than missing the punch line of a joke or a story. Maybe the person telling the joke didn't tell the joke properly, or he left out a vital part of the joke that caused the punch line to fizzle. The person who was listening may have missed part of the joke, or perhaps his understanding of terms was different from the joke teller's, regardless, the joke fizzled.

In order to make the punch line of this thought provoking story, absolutely clearly, may I give it to you in simple, easy to understand language?

An Offer of Full Reward

The senior citizen, who is saved in the biological Eleventh Hour of his life, and who will enter into the harvest of lost souls as his primary purpose in life, will be

> "Why stand ye here all the day idle?" This is referring to people who, through mistakes or sins in their earlier lives, are not active in ministries. They are lamenting over past heartaches or failures. **These are the people Jesus is appealing to in this story.**

rewarded at the second coming as if he had spent all his life working faithfully for

Christ. This reward will entail ruling over part of this earth during the 1000-year reign.

In addition to this group, there is a statement in verse six that broadens this number to include many others. Note the expression, "Why stand ye here all the day idle?" This is referring to people who, through mistakes or sins in their earlier lives, are not active in ministries. They are lamenting over past heartaches or failures. These are the people Jesus is appealing to in this story.

An Offer of Amnesty

In this group described as, "Why stand ye here all the day idle," are many people, who have been saved for a long time, that are nothing more than bench warmers or irregular church service attendees. They do not give a tithe, but just tip the church a little for its services. Most of them who have been standing idle, have never won a soul to Christ, and their unfaithful life as a Christian is a bad testimony instead of a good testimony.

> This thought provoking story is to correct wrong thinking. This thought provoking story is directed to the right people, **the generation who need a second chance.**

Regardless of whether you are in the Eleventh Hour of your biological life, or whether you have been standing all day idle, **the offer is the same,** "Go work in my vineyard by winning souls and **I will pay you as if you had worked all your life for me."**

This thought provoking story is to correct wrong thinking. This thought provoking story is directed to the right people, the generation who need a second chance.

Don't Let Past Broken Vows Destroy Your Dreams

If there ever were dreams that were lofty and noble, those were your dreams at the start. Those dreams were placed in your mind and in your heart by God. They were God's dreams for your life. God has not changed. The need has not changed.

So, you slipped and fell and became soiled merchandise. Listen to the call of the Lord of the harvest, the One who died for you, the One who has never given up on you. Listen to His words. **"Why stand ye here all the day idle?** Go ye also into my harvest."

Don't Let What The Brethren Think Destroy Your Dreams

If there ever were dreams that were lofty and noble, those were your dreams at the start. Those were God's dreams for you too. They represented the abundant life that He planned for you.

You may have fallen. You may have been betrayed. You may have given up or turned aside. But God has not changed.

Don't let what the brethren say rob you. Don't let what they accept, or the standards they demand, dictate to you. Get away from them. Move to another part of the vineyard. They didn't die for you. It is not their blood that cleanses you; none of them gave you life. They didn't call you. **Here is your chance to redeem yourself**.

Listen to the precious One who went down to death and fought the forces of hell for your soul.

Listen to the sovereign Lord of the Harvest. "Why stand ye here all the day idle? Though you are broken, I need you. Though you are not the fresh, optimistic youth any more, I need you. Souls are dying and hearts are crying. Get your eyes off the past. Quit lamenting over things that you cannot change."

"**I offer you amnesty for all your past sins**. I, the Supreme Creator and God, say, Why stand ye here all the day idle? Go ye also into my harvest."

> "Throw yourself into an all out effort to save souls from eternal separation from me, convince them that I love them and will save them. **Use your own testimony of hurt, sorrow and despair** and I will convince them through you."

"Throw yourself into an all out effort to save souls from eternal separation from me, convince them that I love them and will save them. **Use your own testimony of hurt, sorrow and despair** and I will convince them through you."

"We will make a great team."
"The weak and the strong."
"The dumb and the wise."
"The failure and the finisher."
"The soiled and the savior."
"The impoverished and the infinite."
"The hurt and the healer."

"We will make a real team, and **in the end** when I come to my throne, I will remember that in my desperate hour, **you got back up, laid aside the past, and helped me.** If you will do this for me in **the massive, six and one-half to seven billion harvest** of lost souls, I will pay you like you served me all the days of your life!"

"Why stand ye here all the day idle?"

GOD KNEW YOUR PROBLEMS BEFORE YOU HAD THEM

If there ever were dreams that were lofty and noble, those were your dreams at the start. God knew the problems you would encounter before placing those dreams in your heart.

Where did those dreams come from? Who gave them to you? The One who placed them in your heart has not changed.

He knew about your problems, your bad decisions and heartbreaks. He **foresaw them even before you experienced them.** But in spite of those problems, He placed those dreams **in** your heart.

Don't let the devil beat you down. Don't let him laugh at you as he continues to keep you captive. **He has been keeping you standing idle all day long while the poor masses that Jesus died for are lost and dying.**

Hear what the Lord of the Harvest is saying:

- "So you were foolish - I called the foolish."
- "So you are weak - I called the weak."
- "So you are base - I use the base."
- "So you are fearful - I can change the fearful."

ANSWER ONE QUESTION FOR A GLORIOUS FUTURE

My question to you:
- is not – about your past,
- is not – about your status,
- is not – about your ability."

My only question to you is, **"Why stand ye here all the day idle?"**
- I need you.
- Other workers need you.
- The perishing need you.

"If you will help me in my lonely, desperate hour, I will remember you when I come in my power and glory."

"Go ye also into the vineyard and you have my promise for

> My question to you:
> is not – about your past,
> is not – about your status,
> is not – about your ability.
> My question to you is, **"Why?"**

it. On my honor- whatsoever is right - that shall ye receive."
- A new day
- A new start.
- The past is behind you.

THE CALL IS BEFORE YOU

This is your new beginning. He gave you the dreams and your chance is before you now! It is not how you started, but how you **finish, that counts in the Eleventh Hour. "Why stand ye here all the day idle?"**

GOD'S WILL FOR MAN IS TO HAVE DOMINION OVER THE EARTH!

It was God's plan when He created man to have dominion over the earth. It is His plan today, more importantly; it is God's plan for you.

Maybe you have ignored those examples that God placed in the Bible, which were to serve as an inspiration for your Christian life.

Maybe you have reached a comfort level and have eased off in your Christian service. You have accepted the standards of those around you, instead of the zeal and dedication of those in the Bible. This is your chance as an Eleventh Hour Christian.

Jesus has promised you, "Hear my plea for workers, and go to work to help save part of the six and one-half to seven billion harvest; and I will pay you a full day's pay. You will be part of those who will have dominion over the earth. You will rule with me!

"Why stand ye here all the day idle?"

How you respond to his Eleventh Hour plea will have a lot to do with where you will live for 1000 years.

Chapter Eleven
THE PURPOSE OF THE KINGDOM PRINCIPLE

In this chapter, we examine the real intent and impact the Millennial Kingdom is to have upon God's people.

Jesus' offer to his disciples, of a position of honor, near him for one 1000 years, **was to stimulate them to an all out effort** of spreading his message of love and provision to every sinner on earth.

> "And I appoint unto you a kingdom, as my Father hath appointed unto me; That ye may eat and drink at my table in my kingdom, and sit on thrones judging the twelve tribes of Israel." Luke 22:29-30

The offer of eating and drinking at his table and being a king over one of the twelve tribes of Israel was **very motivational**. When the Twelve truly understood the principles of the Kingdom, there was nothing that the devil or the world could do to stop them.

It took the devil hundreds of years to hide the wonderful doctrine of the Kingdom and its motivational effect that God intended it to have upon His children.

In the United States, the devil used the tendency of theologians and the false doctrine of three apostate denominations to keep this brilliant motivational factor obscured.

THE TENDENCY OF THEOLOGIANS

The tendency of most Bible teachers is to **examine and discuss doctrine**. In Hebrews Chapter Six, we see this tendency exposed.

In Hebrews 6:1-3, Paul admonished the people to leave off the discussion of various doctrines and go on to perfection (maturity or fruit bearing.) The tendency of scholars is to study a false doctrine in order to expose the false aspect of that doctrine. When they have this narrow view it often blinds the minds of their readers to the marvelous truth and purpose of the doctrine, which is being corrupted.

That author's purpose was to expose the false interpretation. In doing so, he does not **give a complete analysis of the doctrine**. His writing stresses the errors and when studied by others, they, too, focused on refuting the errors of the doctrine and not the doctrine itself. Most of the time this leaves **the real purpose of the doctrine still hid from the student's mind.**

One of Jesus' the commands to the apostles concerning the Model Prayer was, **"...When ye pray, say..."** (Luke 11:2) In the Model Prayer, they were to pray **"Give us day by day our daily bread."** (Luke 11:3) How could they ask God for daily bread unless **they prayed this prayer every day**? Just as the children of Israel in the wilderness had to gather their manna every day, the apostles were commanded to pray the Model Prayer every day.

> The tendency of scholars is to study a false doctrine in order to expose the false aspect of that doctrine. When they have this narrow view it often blinds the minds of their readers to the marvelous truth and purpose of the doctrine which is being corrupted.

The first item in the Model Prayer concerns the 1000-year Millennial Kingdom. They were commanded to pray every day **"Thy kingdom come,"** which caused them to start every day with their eyes and mind focused on His coming back to set up His earthly 1000 year reign.

This prayer would do two things; it would **take their minds off the problems** of this world and **place their thoughts on the coming Millennial Reign** and their nearness to Jesus.

The vain repetitious praying of the Model Prayer by the people of the Catholic

Church in their masses and funerals cause people to be blind **toward the motivational power, which praying "Thy kingdom come," had on the first generation of Christians.**

THE GREATEST HURT TO THE TRUTH

There are two very prominent cults in the United States today that have spread throughout the world. In fact, the Church of Jesus Christ of Latter-day Saints (Mormons) is among the fastest growing denominations, both in America and in the world.

> This prayer would do two things; it would **take their minds off the problems** of this world and **place their thoughts on the coming Millennial Reign** and their nearness to Jesus.

The Jehovah's Witnesses cult is very aggressive in spreading their false religion. What is their church facilities called? **Kingdom Hall**. It is from these **Kingdom Halls** that they spread their false doctrines, which includes **the denial of the deity of Jesus and hell as a literal eternal place.**

Again, much information has been written refuting and warning people of their false doctrines. In doing so, the truth about the coming Millennial Kingdom that God's children are commanded to pray for, **remains completely hidden and ignored.**

The Mormons are making great strides in our society, which is almost void in real Bible teaching. Many churches and pastors have left off good sound Bible teaching and are completely blind to the purpose of the Millennial Kingdom. Because of the lack of real Bible preaching and teaching in many churches, they are losing members to these cults. Other members are just dropping out of church and are not going anywhere.

The tendency of man is to shut the barn door after the horse has run off, so they teach a series about the danger and false doctrines of these cults, leaving the truth about the Kingdom still unknown.

All of this causes most individuals to be directed toward refuting false doctrine instead of learning the truth, about the coming Millennial Kingdom.

CONTRAST OF MOTIVATIONS

Please consider the **carrot, which dominates the other side of the river.** It will help you to see the tremendous need of understanding and preaching about the millennial Kingdom.

One of the best ways of teaching is to show the contrast between two doctrines. Please consider the contrasting influence between the motivation of going to heaven with the motivation of going into the Millennial Reign.

MOTIVATIONAL INFLUENCE OF GOING TO HEAVEN

Among true believers, **there does not seem to be any motivation** connected to the thought of dying and going to heaven.

The average believer seems to think – "It doesn't matter how I'm living, whether I am faithful or unfaithful in my life to the Lord. When I get to heaven everything will be OK."

May I be quick to add, if a person is truly saved, everything will be OK when he dies and goes to heaven.

These individuals actually seem to believe that they live two distinct and different life spans. One on this earth that ends in death while another life begins after they get to heaven; **this concept is completely false.**

THE SEQUENCE OF A BELIEVER'S JOURNEY INTO THE ETERNAL HEAVEN

Please consider the distinct phases of a believer's journey, which ends **in his eternal home of heaven.**

FIRST PHASE: THE BELIEVER GOES TO HEAVEN FOR A LIMITED TIME.

The word 'death' means separation. When physical death comes, the spirit is separated from the body. Peter referred to his physical body as a tabernacle (tent), which he would put off as a person would change a garment. (II Peter 1:14)

Paul states that when we put off our earthly tabernacle we have a "...house not made with hands, eternal in the heavens." (II Corinthians 5:1) Later in the chapter, he stated, **"...to be absent from the body, and present with the Lord"** (II Corinthians 5:8), which teaches that when a believer dies, he takes **his last breath on earth and the next one in heaven**. The body simply goes to sleep while the real person is released to go to heaven. Solomon explains,

"Then shall the dust [body] return to the earth as if was: and the spirit shall return unto God who gave it." (Ecclesiastes 12:7)

THE SECOND PHASE: WHEN HE COMES BACK TO BE REUNITED WITH HIS GLORIFIED BODY.

At death, the real person (spirit) goes directly into heaven while his body goes back to dust. Apostle Paul explained the second phase of man's journey in I Thessalonians 4:13-18. Read all of those verses, but please note what he said about those **that sleep** in verse fourteen. He said, those that sleep referring to their bodies, **will God bring with Him** referring to their spirit. We have the believers **coming back from heaven and entering into their eternal glorified bodies**

THE THIRD PHASE: TAKES PLACE AT THE SAME TIME AND WILL CONTINUE THROUGHOUT THE AWARDS BANQUET FOR SEVEN YEARS.

Jesus announces this great truth himself in Revelations 22:12, **"And,** behold, I come quickly; and my reward is with me, to give every man according as his work shall be."

Note the expression, "...**according as his work shall be.**" This means that rewards are earned and there will be a difference in rewards given.

> He said, those that sleep referring to their bodies, **will God bring with Him** referring to their spirit. We have the believers **coming back from heaven and entering into their eternal glorified bodies.**

Paul boldly proclaimed, **"And as it is appointed unto men once to die, but after this THE JUDGMENT."** (Hebrews 9:27)

The Bible has always warned each believer of a time in which his life and works will be judged.

"For God shall bring every work into judgment, with every secret thing, whether it be good, or whether it be evil."

In Revelations 14:13, we have the statement, **"...Blessed are the dead** [referring to their bodies] **which die in the Lord...** [because they] ...**rest from their labours**... [on vacation in heaven] **and their works do follow them."** This is referring to the faithful believers who

> Paul boldly proclaimed, *"And as it is appointed unto men once to die, but after this THE JUDGMENT." (Hebrews 9:27)*

died and went to heaven. While they are in heaven, **their works as still increasing** because of the works of the people they won to the Lord. While they were alive on the earth they won and trained people who continued to work for the Lord even after the person dies. These works, along with all their future works, will continue and add to the person's reward at the Awards Banquet.

But alas, the unfaithful believers set in motion (like Lot) some bad or evil works that continue to grow after they die also. Read what Lot's evil works grew into in Isaiah 15. Moab was his son.

It is at the Judgment Seat of Christ that all believers' works will be judged (II Corinthians 5:10) and **tried by fire** (I Corinthians 3:11-14)

It is at the Judgment Seat of Christ that each believer will be assigned HIS POSITION OF SERVICE ON THIS EARTH FOR ONE 1000 YEARS.

THE FOURTH PHASE: IS THE 1000-YEAR MILLENNIAL REIGN

The fact that there will be a one 1000-year reign on this earth has been previously established.

The fact that where one lives for one 1000-years in the Millennium, whether in honor or shame, has been established. Some will share in Christ's glory (I Peter 5:10) while others will weep and gnash their teeth. (Matthew 24:51; 25:30)

THE FIFTH PHASE: WILL BE A QUICK STOP AT THE WHITE THRONE JUDGMENT

The believer will not be judged at the White Throne Judgment. His sins were **judged at the cross of Calvary and his works were judged 1000 years earlier at the Judgment Seat of Christ**.

> It is at the Judgment Seat of Christ that each believer will be assigned HIS POSITION OF SERVICE ON THIS EARTH FOR ONE THOUSAND YEARS.

The White Throne Judgment is a judgment **for unbelievers** and is recorded in Revelations 20:11-15, but the believers will be there, not to be judged, but to witness this awful event.

In Revelations 2:11, the Bible states that the overcomers (true Christians who serve the Lord by faith) will "...***not be hurt of the second death.***" This means that they will not suffer shame or regret and will not have the blood of the lost that are cast into hell on their hands.

But the **unfaithful will weep and gnash their teeth** as they see what their worldly and self-centered lives cost the lost. (Matthew 24:42-51) Before you object to this harsh treatment, consider the eternal suffering of the lost in hell. Also be reminded that God **tried to turn His unfaithful children from their backslidden lives,** but they **wouldn't listen**. In reality, they are the ones who **caused this horrible situation they must live through.**

THE SIXTH PHASE: THEIR JOURNEY WILL NEVER END

Immediately after the one 1000-year reign and the horrible ordeal of the White Throne Judgment of the lost, **comes the eternal home for the saved**.

In Revelations 21:1-5, we have the description of God **making a new heaven and earth.** God, the Father, takes up His habitation with his children in a perfect paradise.

> The final statement, "**and the former things are passed away,**" means that He erases all of the horrible thoughts and memories from their mind. **It is at this point that man passes into the eternal heaven as a member of God's great big happy family**.

Please note that in Revelation 21:4, he wipes away all the tears from the eyes of His children. The final statement, "...**for the former things are passed away,**" means that He erases all of the horrible thoughts and memories from their mind. **It is at this point that man passes into the eternal heaven as a member of God's great big happy family**.

PLEASE CONSIDER THE MOTIVATION VALUE OF THE MILLENNIAL KINGDOM IN THE FOLLOWING CHAPTERS

Chapter Twelve
THE CARROT THAT DOMINATES THE OTHER SIDE OF THE RIVER

The materials for this booklet concerning the Kingdom principles are from the teachings of two renowned leaders in the Apostolic Era, along with a brief word from Jesus. One of these men is the first and greatest pastor that God ever had, apostle Peter, while the other is the humble Paul, who became His greatest missionary. These two men did more to motivate the first century Christians than anyone else.

The senior pastor, Peter, led the first church in Jerusalem to win and then develop between two and five hundred thousand disciples in a period of five to seven years. This feat caused the religious leaders of his day to decla**re, "...ye have filled our Jerusalem with your doctrine...."** (Acts 5:28), meaning they were good, solid, practicing Christians.

The zealous missionary, Paul, almost single handedly, led in the evangelization of most of Europe and Asia. He was also used of the Holy Spirit to pen fourteen of the New Testament books.

These are, but brief credentials of these two elderly statesmen, which we will focus on in order to give **a picture of the carrot that shines so brightly** on the other side of the river. These two spiritual giants of the faith revealed this carrot through their final writings in the twilight of their lives, just before they took their leave for Heaven.

Pastor Peter attempted to motivate through the power of the pen, while missionary Paul attempted to inspire through the example of his life, as God's role model.

The term **"carrot"** comes from the motivational world, and is used as an overwhelming stimulus to motivate people to super human efforts. **Since God created man as a teleological, goal-striving being, it is only fitting for God to dangle a "carrot" before men to stimulate them** to attempt super human efforts.

Man also needed a carrot to help him as he traveled through what would seem to be a "hopeless situation". As this hopeless situation loomed so darkly up ahead in the believer's life, **there was a desperate need for a beacon of hope to dominate his horizon;** this beacon of light would serve to give him joy as he traveled through those dark waters. As men acquainted with trouble and anticipating their soon coming deaths, both Peter and Paul attempted to trim the wicks and stoke the fires of hope and victory as **they prepared to cross over to the other side of the river.**

> As this hopeless situation loomed so darkly up ahead in the believer's life, there was a desperate need for a beacon of hope to dominate his horizon.

It is imperative that this generation catches the vision that these two spiritual giants taught that inspired their converts to such superhuman accomplishments.

PAUL, OUR ROLE MODEL

We will examine the life of one of God's most zealous saints who, as our role model, was stimulated by the carrot on the other side of the river. It is obvious that Paul was motivated to be obedient and pleasing to his Savior, **regardless of personal cost or sacrifice**.

GOD HAS A PLAN FOR EVERY BELIEVER'S LIFE

After a bold statement that sinners are saved by grace, followed by the accented statement that sinners are not saved by any works on their behalf, Paul revealed that every person has a prescribed plan to follow after becoming a Christian. It is written in Ephesians 2:10, "For we are his [God's] workmanship, created in Christ Jesus unto good works, which God hath before ordained that we should walk in them." Again, in II Timothy 1:9, Paul states that each one of God's children is saved for "a purpose," or for a definite job.

GOD HAS A GOOD PLAN FOR EVERY BELIEVER'S LIFE

The loving Father, who gave His Son as our substitute to die on the cross to pay for our sins, has a good life planned for each of His children! Think about it. God, after demonstrating His great love for you by paying that unspeakable price, **must have something special in mind for your life.**

One does not have to depend on reasoning to deduct this truth, because Jesus announced the purpose for His coming to this earth. He said that He came in order to give those that trust in Him life (eternal life), and to **give it to them more abundantly**. (John 10:10) This means that His plan for each of His children is to live a victorious life. Paul stated clearly that God has a **"…good, and acceptable, and perfect…" plan** for each child of God to live. It may not be an easy life, but He promises never to leave or forsake His children. He will always be there to help them.

> "For we are his (God's) workmanship, created in Christ Jesus unto good works, which God hath before ordained that we should walk in them."

GOD HAD A SPECIAL PLAN FOR PAUL'S LIFE

Before Paul's conversion, he was the enemy of Christ and a leader in an opposing religion. Paul, referring to himself before his conversion,

> Paul stated clearly that God has a **"…*good, and acceptable, and perfect…*" plan** for each child of God to live.

said he was "the chiefest of sinners." He persecuted Christians, hunting them down and jailing or executing them. After his conversion to the Christian faith, he became one of God's humble preachers.

God revealed the startling reason He chose (or saved) Paul. Listen to Paul describe that purpose. **"Howbeit for this cause I obtained mercy, that in me first Jesus Christ might shew forth all longsuffering, for a pattern to them which should hereafter believe on him to life everlasting."** I Timothy 1:16

Paul said that God saved him to show what God's grace could do in the life of any sinner who would fully yield to Him. Not only did God save Paul, but He made him a pattern for all those who would hereafter become a Christian.

Paul taught in the Word (Phil 1:29), and showed in his life, that a person should not only believe on Christ, but suffer for Him as well. Paul demonstrated that God's grace is **always** sufficient. (II Cor 12:9)

Paul's life showed that a Christian could be joyful while in prison and, through God's enabling grace, could be more than conquerors in any situation. *(Rom 8:37)* Then Paul commanded his disciples to follow him (imitate his lifestyle), as he followed Christ.

Dear friend, how does your life stack up? How close are you in conforming to your pattern, Paul?

God's plan for Paul's life was to make him a role model for the saved to imitate and follow. Many justify that they are not imitating the life of Jesus by saying, "He is perfect. He cannot sin and I am human and oh, so weak." God's answer to them is, "I saved the worst of the worst and, by my grace, conformed him into a pattern for all future children of God to imitate."

> Paul taught in the Word *(Phil. 1:29)*, and showed in his life, that a person should not only believe on Christ, but suffer for Him as well. Paul demonstrated that God's grace is always sufficient.

THE PRIZE PAUL WORKED TOWARD

To say that the apostle Paul was highly motivated would be an understatement. Perhaps, no other man had the intense focus and drive for Jesus and lost souls as Paul did.

PAUL'S ZEAL MANIFESTED IN HIS DAILY LIFE

Paul told the Corinthians that he commended himself only so they could answer his critics. (II Cor 10:12) He was saying, "Compare my service with theirs and you will see who God's true servant is."

Please note part of his record of suffering for Christ.

"Are they Hebrews? So am I. Are they Israelites? So am I. Are they the seed of Abraham? So am I."

"Are they ministers of Christ? (I speak as a fool) I am more; in labours more abundant, in stripes above measure, in prisons more frequent, in deaths oft."

"Of the Jews five times received I forty stripes save one."

"Thrice was I beaten with rods, once was I stoned, thrice I suffered shipwreck, a night and a day I have been in the deep:"

"In journeyings often, in perils of waters, in perils of robbers, in perils by mine own countrymen, in perils by the heathen, in perils in the city, in perils in the wilderness, in perils in the sea, in perils among false brethren;"

"In weariness and painfulness, in watchings often, in hunger and thirst, in fastings often, in cold and nakedness."

"Besides those things that are without, that which cometh upon me daily, the care of all the churches." II Cor 11:22-28

PAUL SPOKE OF HIS BURNING DESIRE TO KNOW JESUS

Although Paul was a devout Christian, he spoke of his burning desire to know Christ. He said that he counted all of his religious accomplishments as nothing compared to the personal daily fellowship he had with Christ. (Phil 3:4-8) His consuming desire was to totally live his life trusting in Jesus and doing things through Christ's righteousness. Paul stated, **"And be found in him** [Jesus], **not having mine own righteousness, which is of the law, but that which is through the faith of Christ."** Phil 3:9

Paul gave the reasons for his focus in verse Ten.

Paul said, **"That I may know him"** – have a closer relationship and fellowship with him.

Paul wanted to **attain "the power of his resurrection"** – to have a body more like the glorious body of Jesus in the resurrection.

Paul wanted to know **"the fellowship of his suffering"** – endure some of the same pain, suffering and difficulties that Jesus endured while ministering on earth.

Paul desired **"being made conformable unto his death"** or suffer martyrdom for Christ, or die like Christ. Every person must die. The apostles sought ways they could best glorify Christ through their death. John 21:19

The question may have been asked, "Paul, why do you have these burning desires?"

Paul's answer is found in verse 11, **"If by any means** [whatever pain or suffering it takes] **I might attain unto the resurrection of the dead** [That I

> Paul wanted to know *"the fellowship of his suffering"* – endure some of the same pain, suffering and difficulties that Jesus endured while ministering on earth.

may obtain a higher, closer ranking in the resurrection.]"

In the next two verses, Paul stated that he had not reached the level of attainment that his heart yearned to obtain. Because of this burning desire to obtain a closer fellowship with Christ, he stated, "For this reason I am **forgetting those things which are behind** [all of his great revivals and church plantings of yesteryear], **and reaching forth unto those things which are before.**" Phil 3:13

He was totally focused on the future coming of Jesus and in completing the work he was saved to accomplish. This would give Paul a higher position in the resurrection. His exact words were, **"I press toward the mark** [goal] **for the prize** [first place] **of the high** [upward] **calling of God in Christ Jesus."** Phil 3:14

There was something in the future Millennial Kingdom, and a promised position near his beloved Savior for 1000 years, that caused Paul to abandon personal comforts and **endure anything** in order to attain it.

PAUL'S DETERMINATION WAS TO FINISH HIS COURSE WITH JOY

God reveals Paul's purpose. As previously stated, God saved Paul to fulfill a definite work. In Acts 26:13-19, God told Paul,

"At midday, O king, I saw in the way a light from heaven, above the brightness of the sun, shining round about me and them which journeyed with me,

And when we were all fallen to the earth, I heard a voice speaking unto me, and saying in the Hebrew tongue, Saul, Saul, why persecutest thou me? it is hard for thee to kick against the pricks.

And I said, Who are thou, Lord? And he said, I am Jesus whom thou persecutest.

But rise, and stand upon thy feet: for I have appeared unto thee for this purpose, to make thee a minister and a witness both of these things which thou

> There was something in the future millennial Kingdom, and a promised position near his beloved Savior for 1000 years, that caused Paul to abandon personal comforts and endure anything in order to attain it.

hast seen, and of those things in the which I will appear unto thee;

Delivering thee from the people, and from the Gentiles, unto whom now I send thee,

To open their eyes, and to turn them from darkness to light, and from the power of Satan unto God, that they may receive forgiveness of sins, and inheritance among them which are sanctified by faith that is in me.

Whereupon, O king Agrippa, I was not disobedient unto the heavenly vision."

Prophets revealed Paul's suffering and death. Many years of intense ministry had been fulfilled as Paul was traveling toward Jerusalem. He encountered prophets who warned him of suffering, and perhaps even death, if he continued.

"And when we heard these things, both we, and they of that place, besought him not to go up to Jerusalem."

> But none of these things move me, neither count I my life dear unto myself, **so that I might finish my course with joy**, and the ministry, which I have received of the Lord Jesus, to testify the gospel of the grace of God.

Then Paul answered, What mean ye to weep and to break mine heart? for I am ready not to be bound only, but also to die at Jerusalem

for the name of the Lord Jesus." Acts 21:12-13

Paul revealed his consuming desire to finish his course (ministry) with joy. "Save that the Holy Ghost witnesseth in every city, saying that bonds and afflictions abide me. But none of these things move me, neither count I my life dear unto myself, so that I might finish my course with joy, and the ministry, which I have received of the Lord Jesus, to testify the gospel of the grace of God." Acts 20:23-24

THE PRICE OF ENTERING AN HONORED POSITION IN THE MILLENNIAL KINGDOM

Please examine carefully a particular segment of Paul's missionary journey. It will reveal part of the great motivating force of Paul's ministry. The story of this journey is found in Acts Chapter Fourteen.

GREAT SUCCESS IN THE MINISTRY

The apostles were having multitudes saved. Verse one of this chapter states that "a great multitude was saved." God was working miracles through Paul and Barnabas, which brought them and their followers' persecution.

GREAT PERSECUTION AND SUFFERING TO THE SAINTS

As they were preaching, a huge crowd got worked up to oppose the preachers and was soon incited to stone the apostle Paul. (verse 19) He was stoned and left for dead. Soon afterward, he revived and continued preaching and encouraging the churches.

GREAT REALIZATION OF KINGDOM TRUTH

After Paul recovered from his stoning, the apostles **returned to their sponsoring churches** and gave their missionary reports.

One would think they would have been thrilled to report **of the thousands saved and new churches started**. Nothing is recorded about these great victories.

One would think that they would have given a report of **Paul's stoning and the great dangers they faced while preaching**.

Nothing is recorded of their personal troubles and suffering.

What is recorded gives a resounding testimony of what it will take to **have a place of royalty and leadership during the 1000-year reign**. When they got to Iconium and Antioch, they admonished the members to "continue in the faith." That is, do not compromise God's Word! Now, mark the message that the apostles preached to the members, **"...that we must through much tribulation enter into the kingdom of God."** (verse 22) Paul was stating, "If you are going to have a position of honor in the coming Kingdom, then you must be willing to suffer, if necessary, in order to obtain it."

> "If you are going to have a position of honor in the coming Kingdom, then you must be willing to suffer, if necessary, in order to obtain it."

Paul told Timothy, **"If we suffer, we shall also reign with him...."** II Tim 2:12 Paul told the Corinthians, **"For our light affliction, which is but for a moment,** [compared to eternity] **worketh for us a far more exceeding and eternal weight of glory."** II Cor 4:17

As a role model, Paul's life showed that to have a position of leadership and close fellowship with Jesus for the coming

The Other Side of the River

Millennial Reign one needs to surrender to the purpose for which one is saved. Paul, as our role model, reveals that the blessings this committed life brings far outweigh any problems. In fact, Paul's testimony to the Roman church states, **"For I reckon that the sufferings of this present time are not worthy to be compared with the glory which shall be revealed in us."** Rom 8:18

GREAT CHALLENGE: "FOLLOW ME AS I FOLLOW CHRIST"

This was the admonition that Paul gave pertained to the suffering one must endure, as well as the lifestyle one should live in following Christ.

> *"For I reckon that the sufferings of this present time are not worthy to be compared with the glory which shall be revealed in us."*

How did Paul go through all of the trials and suffering he encountered and still manifest a happy, joyful disposition? He was following the example of his Lord. No one ever experienced the pain and suffering **that Jesus endured in His lifetime**. How could Jesus, as a man, endure the

> The way Jesus was able to teach the apostles while living a normal life with this impending judgment hanging over His head was by fixing **His mind on the results beyond the cross**.

cross – the pain and suffering physically, along with the total rejection? That physical suffering was nothing compared to the suffering of becoming sin and enduring the pain of hell. As a man, He suffered the same pain that any other man suffers. As God in the flesh, He foreknew the pain and suffering he had to endure in order to pay for our sins. How could He endure that horrible ordeal that He endured; the sinless becoming sin, the Holy taking upon Himself the deeds of the ungodly, and dying as a sinner dies?

The way Jesus was able to teach the apostles and live a normal life while the impending judgment loomed over His head was by fixing **His mind on the results BEYOND THE CROSS**. Jesus kept His mind on the coming glory of the Millennial and eternal Kingdoms. He looked beyond the cross, with its shame and suffering, **to the results it would bring**.

Paul wrote in Hebrews 12:2, **"Looking unto Jesus the author and finisher of our faith; who for the joy that was set before him endured the cross, despising the shame, and is set down at the right hand of the throne of God** Jesus **focused on the victory** that He would gain through being obedient. **He looked forward to the time** when His Father would give Him His Kingdom, and that he would reign with His redeemed saints. (Matt 19:28)

Paul, as our role model, was able to go through all the trials He faced with the same victory and joy. He was looking unto Jesus, the author and finisher of his faith, **to the time he would join his Lord in close fellowship** as they ruled the earth together.

THE PINNACLE OF PAUL'S LIFE

The pinnacle, or highest experience, of Paul's great life was spent in a Roman prison, where he was executed. Paul was basically forsaken, falsely condemned, and died alone; yet when one reads of his final moments on this earth, he sees **a man who is elated and victorious.** Why was Paul's death the pinnacle of his whole life?

HE HAD FINISHED HIS COURSE IN LIFE

As Paul climbed the mountain of life with his focus always toward his Lord's return, he looked back over the race he had just completed. With joy he exclaimed,

"...I have finished my course..." II Tim 4:7 The intensity of the verbs in this verse gives one the impression that Paul was shouting. He was a victorious Christian that **had been assigned** a difficult task in life, which he had just **completed in victory**.

HE FOUGHT GOD'S BATTLES IN LIFE

Paul referred to himself as a soldier of Jesus Christ. He was a leader in the army of the Lord. He did not use physical weapons in this warfare to save people from hell, but his enemies used physical force against him. He could look back over the beatings, the times in prison for preaching the Gospel, and all the days of hunger and difficulties, and shout, **"I have fought a good fight!** As a soldier, I have been true to my commission. I never turned back or dipped my Lord's colors. I have been His ambassador and stood in the gap to save men from hell."

His heart must have been bursting with joy as he realized that the final battle in his life had been fought, and that he had won. Oh, the shout which must have burst from his lips, **"I have fought a good fight!"**

HE HAD DELIVERED GOD'S MESSAGE

Paul was God's ambassador to the world, with a message from the King. He had faithfully followed the instructions that were laid down in the Great Commission. He had never been intimidated to compromise or water down God's message. He had faithfully delivered the whole council of God. Now, he was facing his departure from this earth. He was reporting in to his captain, who was awaiting his arrival in Heaven, with the absolute assurance, **"I have kept the faith."**

THE PINNACLE OF HIS DEPARTURE

From his lonely Roman prison, we see the pinnacle of Paul's departure from this earth.

HE WAS READY TO DEPART FROM THE EARTH

Paul, referring to his death, stated, **"…the time of my departure is at hand."**

II Tim 4:6   Paul knew he wouldn't go through an agonizing experience of death because Jesus had overcome and tasted death for every believer. Paul looked at death simply as a departure. **He would take his last breath on earth and his next breath in Heaven.** He would see the face of his executioner, who would expedite his departure from this earth, and the **next face to burst into his vision would be that of his beloved Savior.** Death held absolutely no fear for Paul, but gave him a rippling sense of excitement and anticipation.

HE COULD FACE HIS SAVIOR WITH CONFIDENCE

With his battles all fought, with his course safely run, and God's message faithfully given, Paul could now turn his attention to seeing his Savior in Heaven.

HE COULD ANTICIPATE HIS CROWN

The sudden flight into Heaven and the glories he would be engulfed in would cause the time before his coronation day to pass rapidly. We know Paul **was looking**

forward to seeing Jesus and hearing him say, "Well done, Paul, my good and faithful servant." We also know Paul was **looking toward the Judgment Seat**, where he would be crowned.

Paul said, "[Because] …I have fought a good fight, I have finished my course, I have kept the faith…**there is laid up for me a crown of righteousness…**" II Tim 4:7-8

Again, we see Paul as a perfect role model, demonstrating how to handle trauma and death. He was **looking beyond any pain** that he would personally suffer to the time he would stand before the royal courts of Heaven and be rewarded by his Lord and Master, King Jesus. **He even leaves a victors cry of encouragement** to all the following generations of the Lord's soldiers. His cry, referring to a victor's crown was, **"NOT TO ME ONLY, BUT TO ALL THOSE THAT LOVE HIS APPEARING."**

Chapter Thirteen
PETER'S PEN

Because of the various judgments on the world system, angels, and false prophets found in the second and third chapters of II Peter, **the carrot is almost buried from human sight.** Our modern day preachers and scholars are so preoccupied in their search and pronouncement of the impending doom that hovers over our generation that this **life changing carrot** that Peter gives in the first chapter is totally overlooked OR ignored.

In this chapter, we will attempt to uncover this carrot and bring it into the glaring light it deserves by developing a simple outline from Pastor Peter's pen:
- Peter speaks of the past
- Peter speaks of the present
- Peter speaks of the future
- Peter speaks of "an abundant entrance"
- Peter speaks of future unknowns

PETER SPEAKS OF THE PAST
"...give diligence to make your calling and election sure." II Peter 1:10

MAKE SURE YOU ARE SAVED

Give diligence, or make absolutely certain, of your calling and election. In layman's language, Peter was admonishing them to make sure they were saved. In the Bible, when personal salvation from hell is referred to, it is always in the past tense, "saved." **"By grace are ye saved…"** Eph 2:8

The individual is to make sure. Believers are admonished to make their calling and election sure. It is something that each individual must do for himself – make sure you are saved.

Make Sure You Read The Whole Verse.

There are some theologians who wrongfully teach the subject of "election." They teach that the election of the sinner unto salvation is totally of God, and it is God who determines who will or will not be saved. The verse they use is II Thess 2:13, which states, **"But we are bound to give thanks alway to God for you, brethren beloved of the Lord, because God hath**

> *"…give diligence to make your calling and election sure…"*
> **II Peter 1:10**

from the beginning chosen you to salvation..."

Those that wrongfully stress the doctrine of election are quick to go to the original Greek language and point out that the word translated "beginning" means the "casting down," referring to creation. We are just as quick to say, "Amen." It is really referring to

> The answer to this question is simple. God, who is infinite and all knowing, elected the sinner from the beginning **through His foreknowledge**.

the beginning, before the creation of the earth. Then they erroneously argue, "If God chose or elected the sinner to be saved in the beginning, then how could the sinner, who has not yet been born, have any part in his election?"

The answer to this question is simple. God, who is infinite and all knowing, elected the sinner from the beginning **through His foreknowledge**. Peter stated this truth in I Peter 1:2, where he declares, **"Elect according to the foreknowledge of God the Father..."** God can look through time and see the sinner listening to the Gospel and being convicted of his sins by the Holy Spirit. The sinner, realizing he is lost and going to hell, hears of God's love and provision for him through the death of

Jesus on the cross, as his substitute. The sinner then turns from his sins and cries out to God for mercy, pleading for the shed blood of His Son. **God foresees the means** that caused this sinner to call out to God for mercy, **as well as the election itself**.

> God foresees the means that caused this sinner to call out to God for mercy, as well as the election itself.

MAKE SURE YOU DON'T STOP IN THE MIDDLE OF THE VERSE

When one stops reading in the middle of II Thess 2:13, **"...from the beginning chosen you to salvation..."** is the end of the verse, causing confusion and error. **The verse does not stop there;** there is no period after the word salvation. The verse continues on and explains how, or on what condition, God chooses the sinner to salvation. **"...through sanctification of the Spirit and belief of the truth."** It is through the hearing of the Gospel and believing the truth. Verse 14 clearly states, **"Whereunto he called you by our**

> The whole picture is that the infinite God sees the Gospel being preached to the sinner from the beginning, and sees the sinner surrendering to the Holy Spirit's drawing, and thus elects, or chooses, him to salvation.

gospel..." So, the whole picture is that the infinite God sees the Gospel being preached to the sinner from the beginning, sees the sinner surrendering to the Holy Spirit's drawing, and thus elects, or chooses, him to salvation.

MAKE SURE TO MAKE THE RIGHT EMPHASIS

The stress on the doctrine of election is not on **who the elected are**, but on **what the ones who are elected are to do**. In John 15:16, Jesus told the early disciples, "Ye have not chosen [elected] me, but I have chosen [elected] you, and ordained you..." Please note why He chose them:

- **"...that ye should go"** - chosen to go
- **"and bring forth fruit,"** - chosen to bring forth fruit, or win souls
- **"and that your fruit [converts] should remain:"** - chosen to follow up and disciple their converts
- **"that whatsoever ye shall ask of the Father in my name, he may give it you."** - chosen to pray big prayers, "whatsoever."

But Peter, in dealing with the past in II Peter 1:10, stated, "...make your calling and election sure...," or in layman's language, "make sure you are saved" (past tense). As important as one's salvation from hell is, **the apostle Peter only referred to it one time**. In the next few verses, he refers to another principle three different times.

PETER SPEAKS OF THE PRESENT

"...for if ye do these things, ye shall never fall [backslide, or stumble as a Christian]."
II Peter 1:10

Notice the present tense of this verse, "do these things." The question arises, "Do what things?" In the verse, "do" denotes that it is a present or on-going action, and refers back to the principles in verses 5 through 7, in which Peter admonished the believer to add to his personal faith in Christ as his Savior.

> *"...for if ye do these things, ye shall never fall* [backslide, or stumble as a Christian]."
> *II Peter 1:10*

In the growth process, the Christian is to make a diligent effort to build good works into his life and grow into a mature believer, so that he will never backslide or stumble.

Note the process of obtaining God's promise so that, as a child of God, one will never fall or backslide:
- **VIRTUE** - Add to your faith, **virtue** (good works or habits).
- **KNOWLEDGE** - Then Peter continued, "Add to your good clean life, **knowledge**." That is, learn more about Jesus and His eternal Word.
- **PATIENCE** - After taking time to live in and study His Word, add **patience**. Learn to endure and be steadfast in your life of service.
- **GODLINESS** - As you are adding patience and steadfastness to your Christian walk, be sure to add **Godliness**, or holiness. One could spell Godliness, "God-like-ness", which means Holy living.
- **BROTHERLY KINDNESS** - While you are learning to follow Jesus and imitate His lifestyle, be kind to your brothers and sisters. Add **brotherly kindness** in your life because everyone is having a tough time and needs encouragement. Live to encourage others.

- **CHARITY** - While you are practicing brotherly kindness and encouraging your fellow man, be sure to have the **charity** (love) of Christ and strive to win lost souls.

Now, if you do these things in your daily life, you will become a tender, compassionate child of God, who will have real fellowship with Christ.

When Peter encouraged them to add these wonderful, Christ-like traits to their personal faith in their daily walk, **he spoke of these admonitions only one time**. But when he came to the future tense, "<u>**the abundant entrance which will be ministered unto you into the glorious millennial Kingdom**</u>", he did not say it just one time. When he came to the future event of all events for the faithful child of God, **he did not mention it just two times**. Peter repeated himself **three times**!

PETER'S INCONSISTENT CHRISTIAN LIFE MOTIVATED HIM

Why did Peter speak of the future glory and then restate the wonderful promise of future glory a second time? He confirmed that he wanted to hold the coming events of future glory continually before them, even after he died. Why would he be so repetitious?

> When he came to the future event of all events for the faithful child of God, **he did not mention it just two times**. Peter repeated himself **three times!**

First, Peter remembered when all he had to motivate him was his salvation. All he knew was, **"I'm saved."** It was thrilling to know he had eternal life and was going to Heaven, but oh, those ups and downs in his inconsistent life. He remembered his zeal as a young Christian, and his ignorance. He remembered the many times that, through his zeal, he had put his foot in his mouth (figuratively speaking). It was only after he began to comprehend his future position as a king, of sitting and eating at Jesus' table in the Millennium that he began to excel.

Second, Peter remembered when all he had to motivate himself was his spiritual growth. He remembered hearing Jesus teach, and then questioning him as He explained the various parables. He remembered glorifying the truths of the beatitudes as he was instructed by Jesus.

Peter was present during Jesus' great Sermon on the Mount, and later at Jesus' discourse on His second coming. He would always treasure being **chosen and ordained** as one of the twelve apostles.

But, when Jesus was captured in the garden, Peter lost control and resorted to the flesh by cutting a man's ear off. When Jesus was interrogated at His mock trial, Peter stood far off and warmed himself with His enemies. He even denied Jesus, not once, but three times.

When, as the leader, he should have demonstrated courage, he was with the rest of the apostles behind locked doors. Then, he would never forget, although they had already been commissioned to go the world, he returned to his fishing vocation. He remembered the power of his influence, which caused six of the apostles to follow him when he returned to his vocation.

> It made him see how absolutely urgent it was to get the Gospel to every **creature** in the world.

- He was **saved**
- He **finished his Bible college training**
- He **finished his internship under Jesus**
- He was **ordained and commissioned**

- **All of that, and he still failed in his Christian life**

Peter's thoughts went back to when he first saw Jesus in His glorified body. As a young preacher upon the Mount of Transfiguration, he saw Moses and Elijah transformed with Jesus. He was so thrilled that he wanted to build three tabernacles and stay there forever.

But, none of his Bible college training or his intern training under Jesus transformed him into a fearless leader. It was only after **Jesus spent His final forty days** on earth teaching that caused Peter's spiritual growth.

> But it was only after he saw the carrot (future tense), that his life was **changed and his purpose on earth became clear**.

It made him see how absolutely **urgent it was to get the Gospel to every creature in the world.** Without hearing the Gospel, no man would call upon the name of the Lord. Without calling on His name for mercy, no one would be saved from hell. It was Jesus' teaching of the glorious 1000-year reign, where those that gave themselves over to getting the Gospel to a lost world in this short earthly life would be kings. That **caused him to develop his eternal focus**, instead of his limited earthly focus. This focus of being near his beloved Jesus and having fellowship with him each day for 1000 years is what **converted him into being a great fearless leader**.

- **He was saved** (past tense)
- **He was growing spiritually** (present tense)

But it was only after he saw the carrot (future tense), that his life was **changed and his purpose on earth became clear**. His real life would be for a 1000 years in the Millennial Reign, as a king under the King of Kings.

> When Peter saw this truth, he was transformed, and he never slowed down or looked back.

That life could begin at any time, depending on when Jesus came back. Until Jesus' return, he was to exert every effort to winning and training people so that everyone on this earth would at least have a chance to be saved from hell. When Peter saw this truth, he was transformed, and he never slowed down or looked back. His simple job was to preach and train until he was abundantly ushered into the Kingdom, consumed his life.

PETER SPEAKS OF THE FUTURE
"For so an entrance shall be ministered unto you abundantly into the everlasting kingdom of our Lord and Saviour Jesus Christ." II Peter 1:11

This was a promise concerning the future. In verse 12, Peter simply stated that he was only reminding them of something they already knew and were practicing.

> "For so an entrance shall be ministered unto you abundantly into the everlasting kingdom of our Lord and Saviour Jesus Christ." *II Peter 1:11*

Peter's exact words to them were, **"though ye know them, and be established** [practicing] **in the present truth** [about the abundant entering into the coming Kingdom]."

Notice the importance Peter placed on this teaching. Although they knew and were practicing these wonderful truths about the coming Millennial Kingdom, he was not going to neglect to **"put you always in remembrance of these things."**

STIR UP YOUR MINDS WITH SOMETHING YOU ALREADY KNOW AND PRACTICE

They already knew of the coming Millennial Kingdom, with all of the great people of the earth. They already knew that this vast number would be lead by the **KING OF KINGS** and **LORD OF LORDS**, JESUS CHRIST, HIMSELF. They already knew that as King, He would put the devil in hell and peace would reign universally.

"FOR SO AN ENTRANCE SHALL BE MINISTERED UNTO YOU"

Please observe the expression "will be ministered unto you." Peter was saying, "I don't want you to forget, for one moment, the glory that awaits you in the Kingdom. You will be the one who will be the center of attention, **who will be ministered to**."

> You will not have to minister – you will be ministered to.
> You will not have to serve – you will be served.
> You will no longer be a poor, unknown person – you will be elevated to a place of prominence and glory.

You will not have to minister – **you will be ministered to.**

You will not have to serve – **you will be served.**

You will no longer be a poor, unknown person – you will be elevated to a place of prominence and glory.

You will no longer be a person with meager, earthly goods – you will be the boss, living in the big house on the hill. You will be royalty, serving with the King of Kings for a full 1000 years. You will be one of Christ's servants, fulfilling His purpose for your life – **to have dominion over the earth.**

Daniel's prophecy, concerning those who will shine brightest in the Millennium, is for those who were wise in their life. Daniel saw those who were wise as stars shining in the Heavens. Daniel 12:3

Solomon defined a wise person as one who "wins souls." Pro 11:30 So, in order to shine as one of the stars in Heaven, one must be responsible for winning people to Jesus.

WHO IS THE ONE WHO IS MINISTERING UNTO YOU?

One of the truths that make this such an awesome occasion is realizing who the person is that will be ministering unto you.

Is it angels? Could be! Is it other brethren? Could be! The angels and other dear Christian friends could have a great part in ushering you into the glorious Millennial Kingdom. They will certainly be there.

WHAT WE DO KNOW ABOUT WHO IS DOING THE MINISTERING?

The apostle Peter stated something we can know for sure. Peter told pastors that the call of God to His obedient servants was to share in "...his eternal glory by Christ Jesus..." I Peter 5:10

The sharing of "His eternal glory" will be by God's grace, and not by man's brilliance. Peter stated, **"The God of all grace, who hath called us unto his eternal glory."** No doubt, it will take much grace to endure the suffering, the rejection, the trials, and difficulties of a life dedicated to obeying the command of winning souls and ministering on behalf of Jesus. But God attempts to make all of this suffering and pain worthwhile by holding up

> Solomon defined a wise person as one who "wins souls." *Prov. 11:30* So, in order to shine as one of the stars in Heaven, one must be responsible for winning people to Jesus.

the end results before these faithful servants – **the call to eternal glory**, which means one will be elevated to share with Christ tremendous blessings for all of eternity.

WE HAVE THE PROMISE OF JESUS

Jesus promised the apostles that they would eat and drink at His table, and serve as a king over one of the twelve tribes, during the Millennial Reign. Luke 22:29-30

> But God attempts to make all of this suffering and pain worthwhile by holding up the end results before these faithful servants – **the call to eternal glory.**

In Luke 12:37, Jesus promised His faithful pastors who were serving Him when He came back that, **"...he shall gird himself, and make them to sit down to meat, and will come forth and serve them."**

Can you imagine Jesus as the principle one who is taking the lead in ministering to you? One may reason, how could Jesus take the time to personally lead in ministering to the millions of people who will appear at the awards banquet?

> The point is, He has promised to gird Himself and serve His faithful servants. He has also promised to allow some to share in His eternal glory.

As man it would seem impossible, but as God all things are possible. He, as God, will do it the same way He hears millions of prayers now, and personally comforts each of His children at the same time.

The point is, He has promised to gird Himself, and serve His faithful servants. He has also promised to allow some to share in His eternal glory.

THE LONG AWAITED DAY BECOMES REALITY

Finally, the time arrives when faith **turns into reality**. The long awaited day is here and you are ushered into the everlasting Kingdom.

The maestro in charge of the music lifts his hand, and on the downbeat the orchestra and the Heavenly choir begins to sing. You, as the guest of honor, stand. All eyes are upon you. The King of Kings goes to the podium.

The great apostle Paul, or one of the archangels, begins to read the citations and commendations . Then, he turns to face the King and Prince of Heaven and declares, "Your Majesty, it is my great honor to present to you your faithful and distinguished servant…" And with a pause, **he calls your name**.

Prince of Heaven and declares, "Your Majesty, it is my great honor to present to you your faithful and distinguished servant…" And with a pause, **he calls your name**.

The many in your spiritual down-line, whom you won or trained, burst into cheers. **The clapping and cheering is deafening.**

Jesus turns toward you with outstretched hands.

You catch your breath. The crown He holds in His hands…**is your crown.** With trembling steps you move forward and bow your head. He gently places the crown upon your head. You feel its weight settle upon your head. You feel His loving arms around you in a tender embrace.

He speaks, and those words will echo in your mind forever. You will never forget the sound of His voice when he says, "Well done, thou good and faithful servant. Enter into the joy of the Lord and into your kingdom, rule, as my servant, over your subjects for 1000 years."

With His arm around your shoulders, He turns and proclaims, "My Father, members of the royal courts of Heaven, Holy angels, and all honored guests, it is **my**

distinct pleasure to present to you, my loyal friend and servant..."

He speaks your name. The band starts playing and cheers erupt from the crowd.

You are so awestruck that you just stand there motionless.

There is coming a day, and it may not be far off, when something like this scene will become a reality. Peter is saying, **"Now, don't forget it."**

Although the apostle Peter tried to describe the abundant entering into the everlasting Kingdom, his words fell far

> He speaks, and those words will echo in your mind forever. You will never forget the sound of His voice when he says, "Well done, thou good and faithful servant. Enter into the joy of the Lord and into your kingdom, rule, as my servant, over your subjects for 1000 years."

short as you will see when **faith and hope become reality**. For the faithful servants, it will become a reality. **"For so an entrance shall be ministered unto you abundantly into the everlasting kingdom..."**

PETER SPEAKS OF AN ABUNDANT ENTRANCE

"For so an entrance shall be ministered unto you abundantly..."

II Peter 1:11

The Kingdom itself will be glorious – **no wars, no deaths, no tears, no plagues and no monster to destroy the earth.** He will be in hell. He will be chained in hell by the new King, and peace will **reign universally**.

"For the earth shall be filled with the knowledge of the glory of the LORD, as the waters cover the sea." Habakkuk 2:14 The curse will be lifted from the earth. The nature of the wild animals will be curbed and the streets of the city will be safe. Little children will play with poisonous reptiles and neighbors will know and love each other. All of these things will be true because the earth will be governed by the Lord and His proven servants.

Peter wrote of these truths to his converts and believed that they knew and were established in these truths. So, why did he say in verse twelve, **"...I will not be negligent to put you always in remembrance of these things...."**

> The Kingdom itself will be glorious – no wars, no deaths, no tears, no plagues and no monster to destroy the earth. He will be in hell.

Again **in verse thirteen**, he stated, **"I am going to stir you up by putting you in remembrance of these things."**

And then finally in verse fifteen, he stated, **"...after my decease to have these things always in remembrance."**

It is clear that he was trying to pen something for his followers, and all others who become Christians. It was the Holy Spirit's way of using the renowned old pastor, who impacted the lives of millions, to place a **blinking red light** so that future generations would examine his words more carefully.

NOTE THE EXPRESSION: "ABUNDANTLY INTO THE EVERLASTING KINGDOM"

Just to leave this lawless land of death and destruction, and go into the peaceful land where Jesus rules in peace and righteousness, would be indescribable. But it is obvious that the Holy Spirit is attempting to raise our expectations by using the word **"abundantly"** in reference to our

> It was the Holy Spirit's way of using the renowned old pastor, who had impacted the lives of millions, to place a **blinking red light** so that future generations would examine his words more carefully.

entrance into the Kingdom.

We are but men of the flesh. Our knowledge is of the earth and we could travel the world and find examples of things that are abundant, or things that are done abundantly. But in speaking of Kings who God wanted to honor, and in examining past adventures into abundance, there is only one man who comes to mind – **King Solomon**.

What Is Abundance?

When you think of Solomon's construction of the Holy temple – **that is abundance**.

When you think of Solomon's magnificent palace, which took fourteen years to build – **that is abundance**.

When you think of the glory of Solomon's wisdom and rulership – **that is abundance**.

When you hear of Solomon's order and organization, II Chronicles 9:4 – **that is abundance**.

When you hear of the love and joy of Solomon's subjects, II Chronicles 9:7 – **that is abundance**.

> There will be something glorious and in great abundance concerning the abundant entering into the everlasting Kingdom.

A queen came, beheld Solomon's

brilliance, order, riches, and reign, and went away saying, **"…One half of the greatness of thy wisdom was not told me…"** II Chronicles 9:6 – **that is abundance**.

Could it be there are **thrones in the Millennium** that would equal Solomon's throne? II Chronicles 9:17

Could there be palaces built in the Millennium for future kings that would rival or surpass Solomon's?

Could there be joy and honor expressed by your Millennial servants that would equal Solomon's?

This glorious event caused Peter to say it not once, **not twice**, **BUT THREE TIMES** – and to place it in the Holy Bible to be referred to over and over again by men of every generation.

"For so an entrance shall be ministered unto you abundantly."

PETER SPEAKS OF FUTURE UNKNOWNS

When Peter stated, "so an entrance shall be ministered unto you abundantly," he spoke of things that are still beyond this life and, as such, are still unknown. It is clear that, through his teaching, his converts had a clear understanding of what lay ahead in the next dispensation. They had accepted these truths ands were looking forward to the Millennial Kingdom. Peter's intent was to "stir them up," by keeping them focused on the glory that would be ministered unto them abundantly when they entered the everlasting Kingdom. Peter was attempting to help them visualize the crowns that would be placed upon their heads, the rewards that would be given, and the positions of glory and leadership that they would share under King Jesus.

PETER'S DISCLAIMER OF THE COMING GLORY

Peter must have thought that, through his stating and restating and then describing the glory of the future Kingdom, his beloved members and preachers might have thought **he had begun to fantasize the splendor of the coming coronation**. After all, Peter was an old man who was facing death; and old men have been known to lose touch with reality. Peter may have sensed that some would discard what he was stating, so in verse sixteen he made a disclaimer concerning this future glory. He said, **"For

we have not followed cunningly devised fables, when we made known unto you the power and coming of our Lord Jesus Christ, but were eyewitnesses of his majesty." II Peter 1:16

Peter was saying, "I am not overstating the greatness of that coming event. **I am not telling you some fable or fairytale.** I was there on the Mount of Transfiguration and beheld the future glory. I saw Jesus in His majestic form. I heard Him speak to Moses and Elijah about coming events. I am doing the best I can as a poor, frail human being to relate the transforming effects it had on my life. **I am trying to teach you what Jesus taught me.** You are facing dark, discouraging days in the ministry. Soul winning is declining in these days of apostasy we are now in. There are preachers in our own pulpits who are withstanding the truth. There are splits in many of our churches. Liberal brethren, as well as those who have

> Peter was saying, "I am not overstating the greatness of that coming event. I am not telling you some fable or fairytale. I was there on the Mount of Transfiguration and beheld the future glory.

> "With all of these distractions and many of God's people being led astray, it is easy to lose your zeal for lost souls. It is easy to give in to discouragement."

gone too far to the right, are causing much distraction in our memberships."

Peter continued, "With all of these distractions and many of God's people being led astray, it is easy to lose your zeal for lost souls. **It is easy to give in to discouragement.**"

Jesus worked calmly even with the knowledge of the torture that was looming closer and closer casting a dark shadow over His life. Our Lord only manifested love and mercy to those around Him as things got darker and darker. He, for the joy (carrot) set before Him, endured the cross, despising the shame – **"looking to the future Kingdom and the blessings that were waiting just across the river."**

"How did He do that?" Peter challenged.

Peter stated, "That is what I am trying to get across to you. I am trying to do what **He did in His last forty days on this earth**. Acts 1:3 He went over these principles of the soon coming Kingdom – over and over again until it became embedded in our minds and souls."

> We were able to look beyond this seemingly hopeless task by seeing the abundant entrance that would be ministered unto us, into the everlasting Kingdom.

"As Jesus taught the future Kingdom principles, they became a major part of our thought pattern. As we learned and rehearsed these thoughts, they began to become part of our accepted beliefs. Those beliefs grew into convictions. Those convictions were absorbed into our being and became part of us. Now, **they process our being and drive us to obey what were before, hopeless tasks.**"

"We were not overwhelmed by the gigantic task of preaching the Gospel to everyone in the world anymore. We were able to look beyond this seemingly hopeless task **by seeing the abundant entrance that would be ministered unto us, as we entered into the everlasting Kingdom.** We, through the joy waiting for us in the future Kingdom when Jesus receives us home, were able to achieve great victories. We were looking unto Jesus, the author and finisher of our faith, who was waiting for us on the other side of the river. Although He was just beyond the horizon, it seemed like the dark clouds of this world formed a 'V', which centered upon His glorious personage."

Peter's admonition continued, "That is what I am trying to get across to you. By first stating these principles, you were good students and believed them, and began to practice them. But I knew that **I had to hash and rehash those blessed truths** until you could look beyond those dark days **to the abundant entrance that Jesus will minister unto you into His everlasting Kingdom."**

Chapter Fourteen
THE GLORY BEYOND THE SUNSET PICTURES YOUR COMING DAY

On more than one occasion, my wife and I have been all but **hypnotized by a fantastic sunset**. Everything else seems to lose its significance as a beautiful sunset dominates the horizon. At such times, God seems to be showing off His artistic abilities by the changing colors and cloud formations.

On one of those occasions, it seemed like God was drawing our attention to the brightness of the sun, which had just fallen beyond our vision; but the glorious brightness of the sun still dominated just beyond our sight. **A dark cloud formed a "V", which spread out across the sky**. The sun's brightness was in the center of the "V", with colors of orange fading into darker shades until the dark cloud served as a picture frame, giving emphasis to the sun that had just set.

This unforgettable sunset perfectly illustrates what your author is trying to get across **concerning the carrot, which is just beyond the river.**

The river is the end of one's life.

The carrot is the golden sun, which still dominates, but is just out of sight.

JESUS DEMONSTRATED THE PROPER USE OF THE CARROT

Jesus came into this world as a man whose life would pass through the darkness of the cross. On the agonizing cross, He suffered as no other man has ever suffered. He was totally abandoned by both God and man as He took upon His Holy, sinless self the sins of every vile person who ever lived. He died as a condemned lost soul. What made this day even darker was that He was not only man, but God in the flesh. As God, He knew every pain of the cross that He would suffer, **even before it actually happened.**

> The sun's brightness was in the center of the "V", with colors of orange fading into darker shades until the dark cloud served as a picture frame, giving emphasis to the sun that had just set.

How did He endure it? How could a Holy God, robed in human flesh, suffer such shame and pain? He looked down through the narrow "V" to the brightness that lay just beyond the horizon. He saw the carrot just beyond the river.

The Scripture states, **"...who for the joy** [carrot] **that was set before him endured the cross, despising the shame, and is set down at the right hand of the throne of God."** Heb. 12:2

He was able to endure the cross because He looked beyond the river to **the glory and victory that His death would bring**.

He saw the **multiplied millions of souls** His death would save from hell.

> How did He endure it? How could a Holy God, robed in human flesh, suffer such shame and pain? He looked down through the narrow "V" to the brightness that lay just beyond the horizon. He saw the carrot just beyond the river.

He saw the **love and limitless joy** that His sacrifice would bring to those millions.

He **felt the praise and worship** of His grateful children, which would be endless.

The carrot was so much greater than the cross that He was able to triumph in the world's darkest day. **He looked to the gain, which overshadowed the pain and shame.**

Jesus taught this carrot principle to Father Abraham. The Bible records several talks that Jesus had with Abraham. Jesus referred to Himself as **"I Am,"** and said Abraham rejoiced to see His day.

Jesus taught Abraham this carrot principle that

> He was able to endure the cross because He looked beyond the river to **the glory and victory that His death would bring**.

caused him to be able to look beyond life and made him willing to offer his own son as a sacrifice. If God had allowed Isaac to be offered, Abraham believed God would have raised him from the dead.

Abraham was able to **look beyond the river and see the glorious Kingdom** that would come upon this earth. Looking beyond the river gave Abraham contentment to dwell in tents, although he was a very wealthy man, because he saw the city that had foundations

> The carrot was so much greater than the cross that He was able to triumph in the world's darkest day. He looked to the gain, which overshadowed the pain and shame.

(twelve) whose builder and maker was God.

The burning sand, the heat with its discomforts, was nothing to Abraham as he saw the glory that lay just beyond the river.

Jesus taught this carrot principle to Moses. By faith, Moses turned away from a place of honor and distinction in earth's most powerful nation, Egypt, to suffer affliction with the people of God. **"Esteeming the reproach of Christ greater riches than the treasures in Egypt..."**

> The burning sand, the heat with its discomforts, was nothing to Abraham as he saw the glory that lay just beyond the river.

Heb 11:26 Why did he turn away from man's glory to suffer reproach? **It was because God had revealed to him the carrot on the other side of the river. "...for he had respect unto the recompence of the reward."** Heb 11:26 Moses saw Him who was invisible and the coming Kingdom, which gave him faith to face Pharaoh's wrath and triumph over it.

Jesus taught the carrot principle to the apostles. Jesus clearly identified the carrot in Luke 22:29-30, when He told the apostles **they would eat and drink at His table** for a full 1000 years, and serve as kings over the twelve tribes of Israel, if they carried the Gospel to their lost generation.

> Moses saw Him who was invisible and the coming Kingdom, which gave him faith to face Pharaoh's wrath and triumph over it.

In Acts 1:3, the Bible reveals that for forty days He emphasized this promise until the apostles could clearly **see the carrot on the other side of the river**.

The apostles could not be stopped until, through death, they obtained their prize.

Jesus first demonstrated looking beyond the darkness to the glory of the coming Kingdom to the apostles who followed His example of **looking to the joy set before them of eating and drinking at His table.** This transformed them so that they were never stopped by the trials and hardships of their lives. They could see the carrot that was brightly shining on the other side of the river.

> The Bible reveals that for forty days He emphasized this promise until the apostles could clearly **see the carrot on the other side of the river.**

PAUL WAS OVERCOME BY THE BRILLIANCE OF THE CARROT

There are many strange happenings and stories in the Bible. When one finds an unusual happening in the Bible, it is God's way of drawing **the reader's attention to a very important doctrine or truth**. The example of Jonah being swallowed by a large fish is an example of an event that has drawn the attention of millions of people. Balaam's talking donkey is another example. Perhaps one of the strangest stories is found in II Corinthians, Chapter Twelve.

Paul began by recounting something that had happened **fourteen years earlier**. Paul was not sure whether he was dead or alive when this event took place. He referred to the experience two different times. The first time, Paul said the person in the story was caught up into the Third Heaven. The second time, he referred to the Third Heaven (where the throne of God is) as paradise. **He was not sure whether he was dead and really went to Heaven, or whether he was given a revelation of the glories of Heaven.** Many believe that Paul was referring back to the time he was stoned by a hostile mob and left for dead at Lystra.

There is no doubt that Paul's confusion of whether or not he was dead was used by God to **bring attention to the following statement: "…heard unspeakable words, which it is not lawful** [possible] **for a man to utter."** (verse 4) Paul was not saying that he saw something in Heaven that was against the law to talk about. He was saying that he heard and saw things that **were beyond man's ability to talk about**. Man's earthly vocabulary was incapable of relating what he saw and heard.

But the effects of what he heard and saw so excited Paul, and mesmerized his being, that he could not stop thinking about it. It blew his mind, so to speak. The event was similar to the country boy who meets the beautiful, graceful girl and falls hopelessly in love with her. His mind can think of nothing else but that wonderful girl.

What Paul saw had such an effect on him that he could not get it out of his mind. He was star struck. He was consumed by its brilliance and glory.

God, in order to get His servant Paul back to a place where he could finish his ministry, had to demonstrate His sovereign power.

> Paul was not saying that he saw something in Heaven that was against the law to talk about.

God showed his power and control by allowing Satan to afflict Paul with something Paul called "a thorn in the flesh." Please read Paul's very words of why he was afflicted by the devil with something that caused unbearable pain. He said, **"And lest I should be exalted above measure through the abundance of the revelations, there was given to me a thorn in the flesh, the messenger of Satan to buffet me, lest I should be exalted above measure."** (verse 7)

Paul saw revelations (**the carrot**) that were so glorious that he was overcome by their brilliance. The author believes there were two reasons for the very painful condition that came upon Paul.

First, the affliction caused Paul so much pain and discomfort that he had to seek God's grace just to be able to continue his life and ministry. The thorn was so horrible and weakened Paul so much that he had to totally rely upon God in order to continue his ministry. The thorn used by God caused Paul to regain his focus and continue his ministry.

The **second** reason was to show the world that people in hopeless pain and affliction can still overcome **by looking beyond their affliction to the carrot**, which lies just beyond the sunset of life.

What Paul saw and heard caused him to "forget those things in the past" in order to press on to apprehend, or **finish**, what he was commanded to do. (Phil 3:13) He **"pressed toward the mark for the prize."** (Phil 3:14) Something he may have seen in the revelations.

When Paul finally finished his course, by fighting a good fight as a soldier and keeping the sacred trust of preaching the faith, **he was ecstatic**. Dying alone in a Roman prison could not dampen the joy and thrill he experienced as he left this world anticipating **the carrot that was just across the river.** II Tim. 4:6-8

These revelations caused Paul to be buffeted by sickness and pain in order for him to be fully focused on his ministry once again.

> People in hopeless pain and affliction can still overcome by looking beyond their affliction to the carrot, which lies just beyond the sunset of life.

One outstanding message he left to **the millions suffering cruel hardships or devastating pain was A MESSAGE OF HOPE**. His testimony was, "I found the grace of God always more than equal to the task that confronted me. In fact, the fellowship and help I found in the grace and tenderness of the Lord caused me to long for the fellowship of His suffering." Phil 3:10

> Perhaps, instead of questioning God concerning your problems, you should submit to the same grace that lifted Paul to a victorious life.

Dear brother, you may not be suffering pain because you saw the secrets of Heaven, but **God allows suffering to happen in order to bless your life.**

Remember, the Lord offers you the same victories that Paul enjoyed. His grace is sufficient for you also. Perhaps, instead of questioning God concerning your problems, **you should submit to the same grace that lifted Paul to a victorious life.**

PETER WAS AWESTRUCK BY THE BRILLIANCE OF THE CARROT

Peter was so awestruck by the brilliance of the carrot that he could not stop talking about it. Before he could put off his tabernacle, as Peter described his impending death, the Holy Spirit inspired him to write about a glorious coming event, which he had already taught and convinced his converts of.

> If there was ever a need for a carrot that could be used to lift the minds of God's people, it was in the declining times of apostasy, which Paul and Peter endured.

In II Peter 1:12, he stated **"Wherefore I will not be negligent to put you always in remembrance of these things, though ye know them, and be established in the present truth."**

Peter was soon to depart for Heaven. He was leaving his precious followers to face **the darkest hours of their lives**. Gone was the revival described in the book of Acts. Gone were the days of tremendous spiritual results. In II Peter Chapters Two and Three, Peter described the horrible attacks upon Christianity by the devil and his false prophets. **It seemed like the true faith could not weather the onslaughts of the various attacks** that the true churches were encountering. The churches were being attacked from within, by evil brethren who had secretly infiltrated their membership, as well as from without. Their whole society was filled with carnal, rebellious people.

If there was ever a need for a carrot that could be used to lift the minds of God's people, it was **in the declining times of apostasy, which Paul and Peter endured**.

Attendance in the true churches was declining, as people turned to the false churches (described in II Peter Chapters Two and Three). The spiritual climate in the services wasn't as warm, and it was becoming harder to get people saved. The pastors were becoming more like the world.

VISUALIZE THE COMING EVENT

Put yourself in the situation of those disciples, and try to capture the significance of Peter's words. He said, **"For so an entrance shall be ministered into you abundantly into the everlasting kingdom**

of our Lord and Saviour Jesus Christ." II Pet 1:11

Peter had already taught on the subject of the coming glorious Millennial Kingdom, and they believed it.

But Peter could not shut up about this carrot, which was shining so brightly just beyond the river. He had taught them about this great truth, and they had accepted his teaching and were established in it. But he stated, **"Wherefore I will not be negligent to put you always in remembrance of these things..."** verse 12 He continued in verse 13 by saying, "As long as I am alive, I will stir you up by reminding you of the **abundant entrance into the glorious 1000-year reign**, which will be ministered unto you."

Peter, **for a third time**, reminded them of the **abundant entrance** that would be ministered unto them, and stated, **"Moreover I will endeavour that ye may be able after my decease to have these things** [an abundant entry] **always in remembrance."** verse 15

What event was so embedded in Peter's mind that he kept talking about? There was something that both he and his disciples witnessed that **God was using to**

cause Peter to keep rehashing over and over again. Lets continue our study to find the answer.

THE GRAND PARADE OF A VICTORIOUS GENERAL

The Roman government performed a ceremony to honor a general who led his army in a victorious campaign against their enemies. **They gave him a victorious parade through the city of Rome.** On such occasions, the general was clothed in purple and gold, woven in figures setting forth his achievements. He wore **a crown** on his head and held a branch of laurel, the emblem of victory. In the other hand, he carried his staff. He rode in a magnificent chariot, adorned with ivory and plates of gold, which was drawn by white horses.

> Peter kept reminding his followers that they too would be received home (at the awards banquet) as victorious soldiers.

A marching band led the procession after the general's chariot. Young men led sacrifices to be offered in the general's honor, and then came the spoils of war and kings, princes and generals **who had been taken captive.** This was followed by his triumphant soldiers riding chariots. People threw flowers and shouted victorious chants as they went by. Following the chariots, came the Roman Senate, priests, other dignitaries and the rest of the parade.

Peter kept reminding his followers that they too would be received home, at the Awards Banquet, **as victorious soldiers**. They too would be ministered to and honored. But **the abundant entrance** into the glorious Millennial Kingdom **would be far beyond the ability of the human tongue to describe**. Best of all, this unbelievable honor would be ministered abundantly unto them by the One who would be leading the coronation. **It would be their Savior**, who had now been crowned King of Kings and Lord of Lords.

> Jesus said, "The joy, carrot, is so great that you can go through any pain, suffering, and shame to get here. As you travel through trouble, keep your eyes focused on the coming victories in the future Kingdom."

HEAR THEIR BECKONING CALL

Please try to understand what these three great teachers have tried to communicate to us. Visualize them sitting at the Bema Stand **calling back to us across the years.**

JESUS IS CALLING

Jesus said, **"The joy,** carrot, **is so great that you can go through any pain, suffering, and shame to get here. As you travel through trouble, keep your eyes focused on the coming glories in the future Kingdom."**

PAUL IS CALLING

Paul spoke about the all-suffering grace that will far exceed any attack you may encounter from the devil. His message was, **"Do not resist pain and suffering,** but rather accept the grace and fellowship of Jesus as He travels with you in your pain and suffering." Paul stated that, **"For our light affliction, which is but for a moment, worketh for us a far more exceeding and eternal weight of glory."** II Corinthians 4:17

> "Do not resist pain and suffering, but rather accept the grace and fellowship of Jesus as He travels with you in your pain and suffering."

PETER IS CALLING

Peter's reminder, to those who are attacked on every side by a rebellious world of sin and apostasy, was, **"Look to the parade!** See yourself as the one who is riding in that chariot. Hear the chants and the hallelujah chorus being sung in your honor. **Keep that unspeakable and indescribable carrot ever in your mind.** After all, it is just a short distance through this life to the other side of the river."

THE AUTHORS CHALLENGE

> Keep that unspeakable and indescribable carrot ever in your minds. After all, it is just a short distance through this life to the other side of the river."

Dear reader, try to focus and visualize this coming scene on the final page.

On the next page of this book is an exercise that a person should read over several times until it is firmly fixed in his mind. Try to visualize that future scene in your mind. Try to see the joyful faces of some of your family and friends who will be there to share in that victorious and joyful moment. Use that tremendous mind which

God gave you to picture the ceremony **which was designed just for you.**

Turn the page and begin to change your life. It will also **change your address in the soon coming millennium**.

LOOK FORWARD TO YOUR CARROT

Look across the river.
Picture yourself arriving at the awards banquet.
The person who was just honored before you has been ushered off the stage.
Project yourself as being ministered to.
See the honor guard.
Hear the band playing.
Listen to the hallelujah chorus being sung.
Feel the tingling of expectancy in your body.
It is your turn.
Your time has **come**.
There is a moment of silence.
A hush falls over that vast audience.
There is a crown that represents kingship and authority, which is brought to the center stage.
The maestro raises his hand.
Every eye is focused.
His hand comes down.

It is your time.
It is your day.
It is your hour.

Sense it.
See it.
Feel it.

Now, by the grace of God, **go for it!**
MAKE IT HAPPEN!!

IT IS YOUR DESTINY!!!

EPILOGUE
WHERE WILL YOU LIVE ON THE OTHER SIDE OF THE RIVER?

The apostles will **live in and around the city of Jerusalem,** where they will enjoy Sunday dinner at Jesus' house and fellowship with all their heroes, Abraham, Moses and Jacob, **for a full 1000 years.**

Some will live in a distant land **with a pile of ashes** like one receives from a cremation, and lament over a misspent and wasted life **for 1000 years.**

Some will **live with excitement** as they watch their children grow up in a world of peace and security **where the knowledge of the Lord will cover the earth as water covers the sea.** They will see one son wrestle with a little lion cub, while his younger brother lets a copperhead coil around is neck, and feel no fear. They will see their little family grow up and live in a perfect paradise, with King Jesus in charge, **for a full 1000 years.**

Some will live with a fear **worse than death** as they chastise themselves for such poor decisions that wrecked their marriages, families and lives. They will live with a pain that is worse than the pain of death **for a full 1000 years.**

Some will live as mayors of their city. They will live in the big house on the hill, with direct lines to those over ten cities and to the headquarter city, Somewhere, you will live among this vast assortment of people. Ponder the question:

**Where will you live on
THE OTHER SIDE OF THE RIVER?**

About the Author

Dr. James Wilkins is one of five preachers brothers. Together they have preached over 215 years with out any scandal. Dr. Wilkins will begin his 60th year in the ministry on July 16th 2009. he had the privilege of leading his brothers to the Lord.

In addition to this book on the Millennial Reign of Christ he has written several other larger books among those are a study of the Doctrines of Grace, The Model Prayer and doctrinal books. He has authored 43 books or booklets and has over 750,000 in circulation. He is best known for the books on discipleship and soul-winning.

As a pastor or church planter he has helped plant thirteen churches. He hosted his own radio talk program for twelve years.

He is an avid believer in the imminent return of Christ and expects to be preaching when Jesus comes.

He has taught for twenty-one years in Baptist Colleges and has preached or taught over 41,000 times.

He lost his wife, Louella, through her promotion to heaven after 41 ½ yeas of labor. Together they had five children and eleven grandchildren who are active in the Lord's work.

Dr. Wilkins now resides in Espanola, New Mexico with Penny, his present wife of thirteen years. Dr Wilkins refers to Penny as his "Second Blessing". They are active members of the Valley Bible Baptist Church, Dr. Brian McMath, Pastor.

For more information about Dr. Wilkins, his books and ministry visit his website.

<u>www.JamesWilkins.org</u>
<u>leatherman_wave@yahoo.com</u>
505-747-6917

Other Books By The Author.

GOD'S BRILLIANT PLAN TO REACH FALLEN MAN - $9.00

Reveals God's perfect plan or redemption. Presents the Bible method of getting the Gospel to every person on earth in fifty years. This book also shows THE LOCAL CHURCH AS THE TRAINING INSTITUTION which equipped the first generation of Christians to do the work of the ministry. It also stresses the divine power needed to energize God's divine message and reveals the method of personal motivation which God commanded the first generation of Christian to follow which motivated them TO TURN THEIR WORLD UPSIDE-DOWN.

GOD'S CURE FOR OUR NATION - $9.95

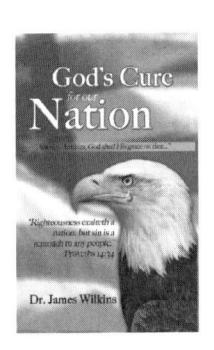

GOD'S CURE FOR OUR NATION TEACHES HOW TO REESTABLISH GOD'S MANDATE TO DEVELOP A VIBRANT BASE FOR TRAINING SPIRIT-FILLED, WORKERS **AND IS DESIGNED TO** CREATE NEW HOPE AND FAITH IN TODAY'S BELIEVERS.

God's cure for out nation SHOWS THE CLEAR STEPS AND SPIRITUAL EXERCISES **WHICH MUST BE FOLLOWED FOR REVIVAL.**

- ❖ SPIRIT-FILLED, COMPASSIONATE PREACHING.
- ❖ PERIOD OF FASTING AND PRAYING BY GOD'S PEOPLE.
- ❖ A REDEDICATION TO THE LORD'S DAY AS GOD'S DAY.

THE SCRIPTURAL GOAL OF TEACHING GOD'S WORD
$6.95

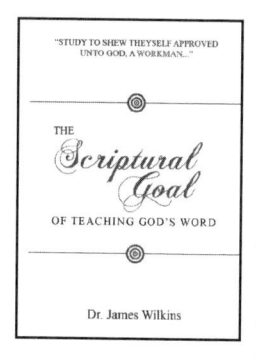

When people "OBSERVE TO DO" **THE BIBLE** a spiritual awakening always followed. When preachers just teach the Word people slowly settled down in their pews and become nominal believers. The spiritual condition in the country would continue to degenerate until people began **to "observe to do" God's Word once again**. Our discipleship and Sunday School books would help get people back to "**OBSERVING TO DO**" God's Word again and help bring revival.

Grandpa, Teach Me to Pray - $9.95

Don't let the title of this book fool you. It was written so that even a child could understand it, but it is **THE MOST GROWN UP BOOK you'll ever read.**

It's thirteen lessons on the **model prayer** which Jesus commanded to **pray every day.** Obeying this command transformed the apostles

from average unmotivated men to men of passion and purpose, which could not be stopped.

MILK OF THE WORD
(24th Printing)
$8.95

MILK OF THE WORD is a spiritual self-help book which will equip the reader to disciple others. It is also a daily devotional which is designed to help the reader learn how to rightly divide the Bible, and is a study course which has changed the lives of thousands! Milk of the Word is now available in spiral bound form as well as perfect bound.

- Rightly divide or study the Bible.
- Establish a prayer time and pray properly.
- Instruction about tithes and offering.
- Instruction in sharing his testimony in soul-winning.
- Honor and loyalty to his pastor.

Mission of The Church -$9.95

MISSION OF THE CHURCH, book two is **the second in a series of four books** in the *New Convert Care Program*, which are designed to develop a new convert (any person) into a mature working discipler.

MISSION OF THE CHURCH, book two, gives the new convert a true picture of what the great commission involves. It will give him greater **vision and purpose** as a Christian. He will learn the simple method which Jesus taught the apostles which transformed their generation. **He will be challenged** by principles of biblical motivation and methodology to become part of transforming our world today.

Meat of the Word - $9.95

MEAT OF THE WORD is the third book in The New Convert Care Program. It has ten lessons on various subjects including: Security of the Believer, Soul-winning, Crowns, The Second Coming, The Holy Spirit and His Filling, and many others.

To Circle the Earth Once Again... - $9.95

Shows the method of training which Jesus used in training the original disciples which circled the earth with the Gospel before the close of the New Testament Era.

Deals with the process of making disciples which in includes two, the disciple or trainer and the discipler or new convert.

Read and find out who the stealth Christian is and how to protect him from self-destruction and danger.

The Mandate...
The Men...
The Method...

Bulk Prices Available –
Now Accepting Credit Card Orders

The Lasting Moments of Joy Series

These are soul-winning experiences which happened throughout my lifetime time but will produce eternal joy.

Stories for dog lovers
Stories for travelers
One story entitled "Is my baby in Hell?"
Another story about the conversion of a Muslim
Stories of the helpless, hopeless who found peace
Stories which both the religious and non-religious will enjoy
The Latest Volume *Favorite Lasting Moments of Joy* is a book about some of the people who have made the greatest investment in my life and ministry. This book is also designed to help young parents build a desire into their children to develop a lifestyle of soul-winning.

The Carrot From Across The River

Have you ever wondered how Jesus could be so calm and collected as he faced the immanent beatings, crucifixion and total rejection he would suffer on the cross?

AS MAN his pain would be just as excruciating as any other man's pain. **AS GOD** he foreknew all the agonies which were about to happen, yet he comforted and instructed his disciples up to the moment he gave himself to die.

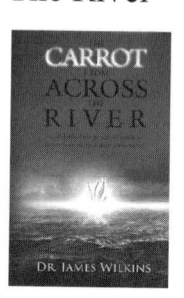

Would you like to know his secret?

How about Paul's secret of joy and happiness, which he expressed while in prison? Abraham, Moses, Daniel and the apostles learned this secret **– LEARN this great truth that transformed them, and it could do the same for you!**

What is the New Convert Care Program

Featuring ONEdisciplingONE

- A BIBLICAL METHOD IN WHICH A SPIRITUAL ROLE MODEL HELPS A YOUNGER CHRISTIAN GROW IN GRACE
- BIBLICAL LESSONS WHICH WILL DEVELOP A YOUNG CONVERT INTO A MATURE CHRISTIAN
- A SCRIPTURAL "FOLLOW UP" PROGRAM WHICH WILL INTEGRATE THE NEW CONVERT INTO THE LOCAL CHURCH

- A SCRIPTURAL "FOLLOW UP" PROGRAM DESIGNED TO AID THE NEW CONVERT TO LEARN TO FEED HIMSELF SPIRITUALLY

- A BIBLICAL METHOD WHERE THE NEW CONVERT STUDIES THE LESSONS IN HIS HOME TUTORED BY A ROLE MODEL

- A SIMPLE "FOLLOW UP" PROGRAM WHICH WILL CUT DOWN THE LOSS OF YOUNG CONVERTS IN ANY CHURCH

  ALL THE ABOVE IS TRUE AND MUCH,

* Denotes Discipleship materials
~ Denotes – Study-to-learn-to-do-series   Special Discounts on Bulk Orders

THE LAYMAN LIBRARY SERIES - $1.75 each
100 * A Letter to a New Convert
102 How to Have Something in Heaven When You Get There
105 Incentives in Soul-winning
106 How to Pray So God Will Answer You
111 Points and Poems by Pearl – Pearl Cheeves
112 Foreknowledge in The Light of Soul-winning
113 Elected "To Go"
114 Predestination Promotes Soul-winning
115 The Ministry of Paul in the light of Soul-winning
116 The Church, a Place of Protection, Love & Development
117 God's Discipleship Plan to Reach Multiplication

$9.95 – Foreknowledge, Election, & Predestination in the Light Of Soul-winning (160p)
$10.95 Essentials to Successful Soul-Winning (258p)
$6.95 Designed to Win (Soul winning Manual) (120p)
$1.75 * From Salvation to Service (also in Spanish) (40p)
$1.75 * How to Be a Better Big Brother (40p)
$1.75 * Big Brother Bits (40p)
$1.75 * Questions Concerning Baptism (40p)
$3.95 * Four Tremendous Truths (55p)
$3.95 * The Mission of The Church (198p)
$3.95 Four Transformational Truths (55p)
$3.95 Healing Words for Lonely People (40p)
$5.95 How To Raise A King (64p)
$7.95 The Truth About Hell (101p)
$5.00 The Final Flight (50p)
$4.95 The Short Race Home (50p)
$5.00 Not Even a Nickel, Just A Penny (Testimony of Penny Wilkins) (40p)
$1.50 A Struggle to Peace (Cindy Benson) (58p)
$9.95 * Milk of The Word – (Book One) (also in Spanish) (146p)
$6.95 ~ Healing Words for Hurting people (120p)
$9.95 ~ The Kindergarten Phase of Eternity (170p)
$9.95 ~ * The Meat of The Word (225p)
$9.95 ~ God's Cure for Our Nation (218p)
$9.95 ~ God's Brilliant Plan to Reach Fallen Man (232p)

All Scripture is from the KJV